A GROUP STUDY GUIDE
Based on the Classic Best-seller by Henrietta Mears

Old Testament

WHAT THE BIBLE IS ALL ABOUT 102

JOB THROUGH MALACHI

A REPRODUCIBLE 13-SESSION BIBLE STUDY ON THE LAST 22 BOOKS OF THE OLD TESTAMENT

Larry Keefauver, Editor

Gospel Light

Gospel Light is an evangelical Christian publisher dedicated to serving the local church. We believe God's vision for Gospel Light is to provide church leaders with biblical, user-friendly materials that will help them evangelize, disciple and minister to children, youth and families.

We hope this Gospel Light resource will help you discover biblical truth for your own life and help you minister to adults. God bless you in your work.

For a free catalog from Gospel Light please contact your Christian supplier or call 1-800-4-GOSPEL.

PUBLISHING STAFF
William T. Greig, Publisher
Dr. Elmer L. Towns, Senior Consulting Publisher
Dr. Gary S. Greig, Senior Consulting Editor
Larry Keefauver, Editor
Jean Daly, Managing Editor
Pam Weston, Editorial Assistant
Kyle Duncan, Associate Publisher
Bayard Taylor, M.Div., Editor, Theological and Biblical Issues
Debi Thayer, Designer

ISBN 0-8307-1797-8

HOW TO MAKE CLEAN COPIES
FROM THIS BOOK

YOU MAY MAKE COPIES OF PORTIONS OF THIS BOOK WITH A CLEAN CONSCIENCE IF:
- you (or someone in your organization) are the original purchaser;
- you are using the copies you make for a noncommercial purpose (such as teaching or promoting your ministry) within your church or organization;
- you follow the instructions provided in this book.

HOWEVER, IT IS ILLEGAL FOR YOU TO MAKE COPIES IF:
- you are using the material to promote, advertise or sell a product or service other than for ministry fund-raising;
- you are using the material in or on a product for sale;
- you or your organization are **not** the original purchaser of this book.

By following these guidelines you help us keep our products affordable.
Thank you,
Gospel Light

CONTENTS

Contents

To complete this course in 11 sessions combine Sessions 10 and 11 and combine Sessions 12 and 13.

WHAT THIS COURSE IS ABOUT

God's Word is vibrant and alive, and His plan for our lives is contained between the pages of His book—the Bible. Everything we need to know about living in wholeness is contained within the pages of His Word. Yet we sometimes forget that the Bible is more than a series of unrelated, independent books—it is a connected, all-encompassing, interwoven work that provides a panoramic view of His love and plan for us.

However, the average person knows little about the Bible. Very few have a comprehensive idea of the whole book. We need, besides a microscopic study of individual books, chapters and verses, a telescopic study of God's Word in order to better understand His plan of salvation and movement in our lives. Through this study, you and your group will be able to see the interconnection between the Old and New Testaments, between the prophets and Christ. You will also see how Jesus Christ is portrayed in each book of the Bible.

The Bible is a collection of 66 books written by at least 40 authors over a period of about 1,600 years. To help us gain an accurate perspective of this monumental work, we will be using the best-selling Bible study resource *What the Bible Is All About* by Henrietta C. Mears. This book provides helpful summaries of each book of the Bible, helping us to see the common threads of good news from beginning to end.

As we begin this exploration, we must keep in mind that sometimes the Bible gives a great deal of detail, while at other times there are only brief statements. However, gaining the perspective of the Bible's major events and characters provides a helpful mental map in which to locate and understand the great riches the Book contains.

"The Bible is one book, one history, one story, His story. Behind the 10,000 events stands God, the builder of history, the maker of the ages. Eternity bounds the one side, eternity bounds the other side, and time is in between: Genesis—origins, Revelation—endings, and all the way between, God is working things out. You can go down into the minutest detail everywhere and see that there is one great purpose moving through the ages: the eternal design of the Almighty God to redeem a wrecked and ruined world" (*What the Bible Is All About* by Henrietta Mears, page 20).

In this course, *What the Bible Is All About 102 Old Testament: Job—Malachi*, group members study the book of Job through the book of Malachi. God's workings and revelations are discovered while seeing how Jesus Christ is portrayed in each of these books of the Bible.

THIS GROUP STUDY GUIDE

This group study guide is a unique companion to *What the Bible Is All About*, offering a stimulating and enjoyable opportunity for group study of the whole Bible and its most important events and characters.

This group study guide is unique because it:

- Is based on the premise that a study of the Bible's most important events and characters is truly an exciting adventure of great value for everyone: novices and scholars, believers and seekers, male and female;

- Organizes the vast span of Bible history into four sections and the major events and characters for each section;

- Provides useful handles for looking into the meaning of historical events, identifying the greatest fact and the greatest truth for each period of Bible history;

- Includes comprehensive One-Year and Two-Year Bible Study Plans for individual study or group study after completing the course overview;

- Requires very few additional supplies for class sessions. (An overhead projector is helpful, but not necessary. Blank paper, index cards, pencils and felt-tip pens are typical of the easily secured materials, which help add variety and stimulate involvement. Suggested supplies are listed at the beginning of each session.)

- Suggests individual reading assignments to review each session, adding further reinforcement to each person's learning.

SESSION PLAN

Each of the 13 sessions is flexibly designed to be completed in one of two time schedules:

Option A—60-minute sessions.

Option B—90-minute sessions.

You will find instructions placed in boxes and marked with the following clock symbol. This information provides optional learning experiences to extend the session to accommodate a 90-minute session.

OPTION ONE

This option will add 15 minutes to the session. These optional activities explore aspects of the main point that could not be addressed in the shorter time schedules.

OPTION TWO

This option will add 15 minutes to the session. These optional activities explore aspects of the main point that could not be addressed in the shorter time schedules.

A FEW TEACHING TIPS

1. Keep It Simple. Teaching people about the Old Testament can seem like an overwhelming task. The Old Testament contains a vast amount of highly interesting, deeply meaningful information. Avoid trying to pass all of this information on to your eager learners. Participants will remember far more if you keep the focus on one issue at a time, seeking to keep your explanations as brief and simple as possible.

2. Keep It Light. Some of the session introductory activities in this manual are fun! This is intentional. Many people who most need this course are intimidated by the Bible. Often there is fear that their own lack of knowledge will be exposed. People who are intimidated and fearful are not ready to learn. The light-hearted approaches are devices to help people relax so they can learn efficiently.

3. Keep It Significant. Because the course has some light touches does not mean its content can be handled frivolously. Keep clearly in mind—and repeatedly emphasize with your class—that this course is dealing with God's plan as it is revealed in the whole Bible. The insights gained in these sessions can make a big difference, not just through their increased understanding of the whole Bible, but in seeing how God's Word applies to their own lives.

4. Keep It Interactive. The learning activities in this manual provide a variety of involving experiences, recognizing the various learning styles which will be present in any group of adults. While some of the activities may not fit your preferred

teaching style, by using this varied path to learning, you make sure that those who learn differently from the way you do will also have their needs met. A common type of involvement is having people share some of their experiences, helping one another expand their understandings of how God works in a variety of ways in our lives.

5. Keep It Prayerful. Both in your preparation and in each class session, pray earnestly that you and your class will be open to the truths of the Old Testament which must be real to us if we are to enrich and deepen our relationship with God. To capture the interest of people in this course:

- Share some of your own experiences with God's Word. To succeed in leading this course, you do not need to be an expert on theology, on the Bible or on teaching methods. You do need to be honest about some of your struggles in seeking to understand and/or explain the Bible.

- Point out that while societies and cultures change, and many life experiences are different for people today than for any preceding generation, God's desire for relationship with His people has remained constant in all of human history.

- Allow people to think and talk about their own experiences with God's Word. Many adults struggle with understanding and studying the Bible, finding it difficult, an obligation that causes feelings of guilt for not achieving what they feel they are expected to. This course is not a therapy workshop, but there is great value in allowing people to be open and honest in expressing their struggles. Admission of a problem is the first step in making progress toward growth.

ALTERNATE SESSION PLANS

OPTIONS FOR USING THE FOUR *WHAT THE BIBLE IS ALL ABOUT* GROUP STUDY GUIDES

Bible Overview (Eight Sessions):

What the Bible Is All About 101 Old Testament: Genesis—Esther Session 2—Genesis to Joshua

What the Bible Is All About 101 Old Testament: Genesis—Esther Session 8—Judges to Esther

What the Bible Is All About 102 Old Testament: Job—Malachi Session 1—Job to Song of Solomon

What the Bible Is All About 102 Old Testament: Job—Malachi Session 5—Isaiah to Malachi

What the Bible Is All About 201 New Testament: Matthew—Philippians Session 1—The Four Gospels

What the Bible Is All About 201 New Testament: Matthew—Philippians Session 6—Acts to Philippians

What the Bible Is All About 202 New Testament: Colossians—Revelation Session 1—Colossians to Philemon

What the Bible Is All About 202 New Testament: Colossians—Revelation Session 8—Hebrews to Revelation

Foundations of Christianity/New Christians (13 Sessions):

What the Bible Is All About 101 Old Testament: Genesis—Esther Session 2—Genesis to Joshua

What the Bible Is All About 101 Old Testament: Genesis—Esther Session 8—Judges to Esther

What the Bible Is All About 102 Old Testament: Job—Malachi Session 1—Job to Song of Solomon

What the Bible Is All About 102 Old Testament: Job—Malachi Session 5—Isaiah to Malachi

What the Bible Is All About 201 New Testament: Matthew—Philippians Session 1—The Four Gospels

What the Bible Is All About 201 New Testament: Matthew—Philippians Session 6—Acts to Philippians

What the Bible Is All About 202 New Testament: Colossians—Revelation Session 1—Colossians to Philemon

What the Bible Is All About 202 New Testament: Colossians—Revelation Session 8—Hebrews to Revelation

What the Bible Is All About 201 New Testament: Matthew—Philippians Session 2—Matthew

What the Bible Is All About 201 New Testament: Matthew—Philippians Session 5—John

What the Bible Is All About 201 New Testament: Matthew—Philippians Session 8—Romans

What the Bible Is All About 201 New Testament: Matthew—Philippians Session 12—Ephesians

What the Bible Is All About 102 Old Testament: Job—Malachi Session 3—Psalms

Bible Overview with Old Testament Emphasis (13 Sessions):

What the Bible Is All About 101 Old Testament: Genesis—Esther Session 2—Genesis to Joshua

What the Bible Is All About 101 Old Testament: Genesis—Esther Session 8—Judges to Esther

What the Bible Is All About 102 Old Testament: Job—Malachi Session 1—Job to Song of Solomon

What the Bible Is All About 102 Old Testament: Job—Malachi Session 5—Isaiah to Malachi

What the Bible Is All About 201 New Testament: Matthew—Philippians Session 1—The Four Gospels

What the Bible Is All About 201 New Testament: Matthew—Philippians Session 6—Acts to Philippians

What the Bible Is All About 202 New Testament: Colossians—Revelation Session 1—Colossians to Philemon

What the Bible Is All About 202 New Testament: Colossians—Revelation Session 8—Hebrews to Revelation

What the Bible Is All About 101 Old Testament: Genesis—Esther Session 4—Exodus

What the Bible Is All About 101 Old Testament: Genesis—Esther Session 10—1 Samuel

What the Bible Is All About 102 Old Testament: Job—Malachi Session 3—Psalms

What the Bible Is All About 102 Old Testament: Job—Malachi Session 9—Daniel

What the Bible Is All About 102 Old Testament: Job—Malachi Session 11—Obadiah, Jonah and Micah

Bible Overview with New Testament Emphasis (13 Sessions):

What the Bible Is All About 101 Old Testament: Genesis—Esther Session 2—Genesis to Joshua

What the Bible Is All About 101 Old Testament: Genesis—Esther Session 8—Judges to Esther

What the Bible Is All About 102 Old Testament: Job—Malachi Session 1—Job to Song of Solomon

What the Bible Is All About 102 Old Testament: Job—Malachi Session 5—Isaiah to Malachi

What the Bible Is All About 201 New Testament: Matthew—Philippians Session 1—The Four Gospels

What the Bible Is All About 201 New Testament: Matthew—Philippians Session 6—Acts to Philippians

What the Bible Is All About 202 New Testament: Colossians—Revelation Session 1—Colossians to Philemon

What the Bible Is All About 202 New Testament: Colossians—Revelation Session 8—Hebrews to Revelation

What the Bible Is All About 201 New Testament: Matthew—Philippians Session 2—Matthew

What the Bible Is All About 201 New Testament: Matthew—Philippians Session 5—John

What the Bible Is All About 201 New Testament: Matthew—Philippians Session 7—Acts

What the Bible Is All About 201 New Testament: Matthew—Philippians Session 8—Romans

What the Bible Is All About 202 New Testament: Matthew—Philippians Session 12—Ephesians

FOR 11-SESSION COURSES

What the Bible Is All About 101 Old Testament: Genesis—Esther:
Combine Sessions 5 and 6; combine Sessions 10 and 11.

What the Bible Is All About 102 Old Testament: Job—Malachi:
Combine Sessions 10 and 11; combine Sessions 12 and 13.

What the Bible Is All About 201 New Testament: Matthew—Philippians:
Combine Sessions 9 and 10; combine Sessions 12 and 13.

What the Bible Is All About 202 New Testament: Colossians—Revelation:
Combine Sessions 3 and 4; combine Sessions 5 and 6.

Previewing Job Through Song of Solomon

The purpose of this session is:

- To provide an overview of the themes of Job through the Song of Solomon;
- To discover how Jesus Christ is revealed in these books as God's Wisdom.

In this session, group members will learn:

- Key truths from favorite verses about God's story in Job through Song of Solomon;
- That Jesus Christ is revealed in Job through Song of Solomon;
- The basic principle that true wisdom is viewing life from God's perspective rather than our own;
- How to apply basic truths about wisdom from these books to their own lives.

KEY VERSES

"I know that my Redeemer lives, and that in the end he will stand upon the earth. And after my skin has been destroyed, yet in my flesh I will see God; I myself will see him with my own eyes—I, and not another. How my heart yearns within me!" Job 19:25-27

"Praise the LORD. Sing to the LORD a new song, his praise in the assembly of the saints." Psalm 149:1

"Blessed is the man who finds wisdom, the man who gains understanding." Proverbs 3:13

"Fear God and keep his commandments, for this is the whole duty of man." Ecclesiastes 12:13

"He has taken me to the banquet hall, and his banner over me is love." Song of Solomon 2:4

BEFORE THE SESSION

- Pray for group members by name, asking the Holy Spirit to teach them the spiritual truths in these books.
- Read chapter 26 and skim chapters 15-17 in *What the Bible Is All About*.

- Prepare copies of the Session 1 handout "Previewing God's Story in Job Through Song of Solomon" for group members.
- Check off these supplies once you have secured them:
  - ____ Name tags for group members;
  - ____ A chalkboard and chalk or a flip chart or an overhead projector with markers;
  - ____ Crayons and blank paper;
  - ____ Extra Bibles, pencils and paper for group members who need them.
- If you are having a 90-minute session, carefully read the two option sections right now and pull together any supplies you will need for them.
- Read the entire session and look up every passage. Have your Bible *Tuck-In*™ page ready for yourself.
- Arrive early and be ready to warmly greet each group member as he or she arrives.
- Memorize the key verses. Share them periodically and ask the group to repeat them as you teach the session.

SECTION ONE: GOD'S STORY (20 MINUTES)

THE WRITINGS: WISDOM AND SONGS FOR ALL OF LIFE

Objective: To preview God's Story in the wisdom literature of the Old Testament.

Greet everyone and give everyone a name tag as they arrive. Form a circle with the chairs and have everyone be seated. Invite volunteers to share their completions to the following:

One thing that I learned from studying Genesis through Esther was _____.

Distribute the handout "Previewing God's Story in Job Through Song of Solomon" to group members. Tell the following story, doing the suggested activities as you come to them.

God spoke to His people by revealing His wisdom and songs to Israel.

In the first few months of our study, we have heard God's Story in the books of law and history. In the upcoming study, we will explore the books of wisdom, called "the writings," and the prophets. Today we are previewing the wisdom literature of Israel—Job through the Song of Solomon. Let's begin by finding out what wisdom is.

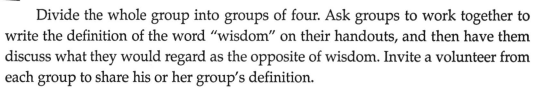

Divide the whole group into groups of four. Ask groups to work together to write the definition of the word "wisdom" on their handouts, and then have them discuss what they would regard as the opposite of wisdom. Invite a volunteer from each group to share his or her group's definition.

Tell the members of each small group to divide up the following verses among themselves, look them up, read them and then summarize what their assigned verses say about wisdom to their other group members: Job 28:12-28; 38:36,37; Psalms 37:30,31; 51:6; 111:10; Proverbs 2:1-6; 4:5-12; 9:10; 24:3; Ecclesiastes 1:16-18; 7:11,12; 9:13-18; 10:12. Then have them complete the following statements on their handouts:

God's wisdom is _____.

We are to acquire wisdom because _____.

After everyone has completed their sentences, invite them to share what they have written with their small groups. Then ask each small group to arrive at a consensus among themselves on how they would complete those sentences as a group. Have the small groups share their group's sentence completions with the whole group.

In Hebrew the main word for God's wisdom is *chokmah* which means "wisdom, skill, willingness to be taught." It is the ability to apply God's will to specific situations.

The wisdom literature in the Old Testament helps us see ourselves and all of life from God's perspective rather than our own. For example, we may see our enemies as prospering, but God knows that their end is destruction (see Proverbs 2—3).

Give paper and crayons to each small group of four. Invite them to draw a picture of you, their group leader. Then show the group a photo of yourself. Compare that photo of yourself with what the group members have drawn. Have some fun with this and then explain: **The photograph represents God's wisdom. Your pictures of me are not as accurate or detailed as the photograph. No matter where other perspectives may come from, they are not as accurate as God's perspective. The only clear and accurate view of reality is found in God's wisdom.**

Job's friends tried to interpret why he was suffering. Only God in His wisdom knew the whole picture.

Let's preview Job. Satan believed that Job was upright before God only because he was prospering. *Take away Job's blessings and he will curse God*, thought Satan. God allowed Satan to take Job's wealth, family and health. Job continued to worship God, but his friends believed that his suffering must have occurred because of sin in Job's life. Job questioned God, wanting an explanation for the universal question—why must I suffer so? Satan, Job's friends and even Job himself did not have the wisdom to understand God's ways (see Job 1—11).

One perspective that we learn from the wisdom literature is that man's wisdom falls far short of understanding God's ways. In the small groups, have the members discuss the following questions:

What is one mystery about God that you cannot understand?

Give an example from your life of a time when it took months or even years for you to understand God's wisdom in a difficult situation in your life.

In the psalms, God is described in many ways: He is our Strength, Fortress and Rock who protects us (see Psalm 18); He is our loving Shepherd who guides us through life's difficulties even when present circumstances seem impossible (see Psalm 23).

Over and over again the psalmists question God, only to learn that His ways are the only way to face life's difficulties and joys.

In previewing the psalms, tell the group that they will discover some of the deep, searching questions the psalmists raised when they lacked wisdom and understanding of God's ways. Assign the following verses to various group members: Psalms 3:1,2; 4:1; 6:3; 10:1; 13:1,2; 22:1; 24:3; 28:1; 38:1-4; 42:1,2; 43:1,2; 44:23-26; 51:10,11; 94:3; 102:1. As they read these questions or cries to God from the psalms, you will list their findings on the board, overhead or flip chart.

Have everyone return to their small groups and ask them to share any question or cry they may have asked over the past year and how God responded to that question or cry.

In Proverbs, God desires for us to seek His wisdom and understanding. Repeatedly Proverbs declares that the fear—respect, awe and honor—of the Lord is the beginning of knowledge, understanding and wisdom.

Without God's wisdom, Proverbs reveals that our families, marriages, relationships and prosperity are all in jeopardy (see Proverbs 2—3).

Ask the small groups to assign seven or eight chapters of Proverbs to each person in their group to be quickly skimmed. Tell them to jot down three or four things on their handouts that they find in their assigned chapters about wisdom—about living life God's way and not according to human wisdom. Then have each person share what they have discovered about wisdom with the others in their group.

In Ecclesiastes, human wisdom and knowledge not centered in God is declared to be meaningless while true wisdom is to fear Him and keep His commandments (see Ecclesiastes 12:13,14).

With the whole group, discuss the following:

What is foolish about pursuing wealth, education or status in the world?

What are the differences you see between God's wisdom and worldly wisdom?

The Song of Solomon describes the wonderful and sometimes mysterious relationship of love between a husband and wife. This beautiful book has also been interpreted as describing the love relationship God has with His people (see Song of Solomon 1).

Discuss how God's perspective on love is different from the world's. List the differences on a chalkboard, overhead or flip chart.

These books filled with the wisdom of God are called "the wisdom writings or wisdom literature."

Remember this simple definition—true wisdom, knowledge and understanding is seeing life from God's perspective and not our own.

Perhaps the verse that sums this up best is found in Proverbs 14:12 and 16:25: "There is a way that seems right to a man, but in the end it leads to death."

OPTION ONE: (FOR A 90-MINUTE SESSION)

God Is My Strength and Refuge (15 Minutes)

Say: **One of the most compelling truths throughout the wisdom writings in the Old Testament is that real safety, strength, refuge and protection can be found nowhere else but in God. All other things in this world fail us except God. True wisdom is knowing that you must put your trust in the Lord.**

Divide the group into six smaller groups. Assign the following passages to each of the groups.

Group One:	Job 13:15; 19:25-27
Group Two:	Psalm 23:1-6
Group Three:	Psalms 46:1-3; 55:22; 56:9-11
Group Four:	Psalm 91:1-6
Group Five:	Proverbs 2:12; 3:5,6
Group Six:	Ecclesiastes 2:24-26; 3:9-12

Ask them to read their assigned passages and then write their completion for the following statement on their handouts:

God is my refuge and strength when _____.

SECTION TWO: GOD'S PERSON (20 MINUTES)

THE BLESSED PERSON: ONE WHO IS WISE

Objective: To learn that God blesses the wise.

Say: **The biblical person we are studying in this lesson is not a particular individual from biblical history, but the person that God desires us to be—the one highlighted for us throughout the wisdom literature. We might study Solomon as a person of wisdom, yet he was only wise early in his reign as king of Israel. The qualities of wise living identified in these books are a model for all believers. Let's identify the essentials of wisdom for living a blessed life in the Lord.**

Divide the whole group into four smaller groups. The handout section "The Blessings of Wisdom" will guide each group in looking at their passage and discovering how being wise in God will bless a believer.

After each group has spent about ten minutes going through their passages, bring the whole group back together and discuss:

What is required of the person who desires to be wise in the ways of God?

What blessings are available to the righteous?

With the whole group complete the following one-sentence description:

The person wise in God's ways is _____.

OPTION TWO: (FOR A 90-MINUTE SESSION)

Heart and Tongue Matters (15 Minutes)

Say: **A key theme in Proverbs is the heart of a person. For the ancient Hebrews, the heart is the central focus of a person's inner self. In the heart, decisions are made and the deepest spiritual matters are pondered. The direction of one's heart sets the course of a person's life. How the heart expresses itself is through the tongue. So the tongue reveals what's in one's heart.**

Ask everyone in the group to turn to the book of Proverbs. Divide the whole group into two groups—the "tongue group" and the "heart group." Ask each group to divide the chapters of Proverbs between its members and then to skim through the chapters looking for every reference to their subject. Have each group appoint a recorder who will jot down what each reference says about the heart or the tongue. Each group has seven minutes to find their references and write down the descriptions that they discover.

After both groups have completed their lists, ask the recorders to write their lists on the board. Then have a group discussion on the following questions:

How are wise children of God supposed to guard their hearts?

What should our tongues express?

What should we keep from our tongues?

SECTION THREE: GOD'S SON (10 MINUTES)

JESUS CHRIST REVEALED AS GOD'S WISDOM

Objective: To discover how Jesus is revealed in the wisdom literature.

Of course, one central theme of these writings is God's wisdom. In the New Testament, Jesus is revealed as our Wisdom: "but to those whom God has called, both Jews and Greeks, Christ the power of God and the wisdom of God" (1 Corinthians 1:24).

Read John 1:1-5 to the group. Ask the group members to find a partner. In each pair, ask that one partner read the odd-numbered verses and the other read the even-numbered verses of Proverbs 4 together. Each time the reader comes across the word "wisdom" or a personal pronoun like "I," "me" or "my," he or she is to substitute the word "Jesus" or "Christ." After they complete this responsive reading, discuss the following with the whole group:

Which parts of Proverbs 4 sound the most like Jesus' ministry?

In what ways did Jesus embody Old Testament wisdom?

PURSUING GOD (5 MINUTES)

NEXT STEPS I NEED TO TAKE

Objective: To take a realistic assessment of one's relationship with Jesus and how that relationship might grow closer in the coming week.

Ask the group members to remain in their pairs. Have each group member list five qualities of wisdom on the handout that he or she needs in his or her own life.

Once they have completed their lists, ask them to share those qualities with their partners and to prioritize them from the most to the least needed.

Ask each group member to complete the following sentence for his or her partner: **Jesus Christ is my Wisdom when He _____.**

PRAYER (5 MINUTES)

PRAYING FOR WISDOM

Objective: To close the session with a deeper desire to have God's perspective or wisdom guiding one's life.

Have the whole group form a circle. Identify three areas in which they might pray for wisdom:

 In their families and/or marriages;

 In their church;

 In the country.

Ask volunteers to say a sentence prayer for wisdom in one of these areas of life. As the leader, close the prayer time asking God to give each person God's wisdom.

PREVIEWING JOB THROUGH SONG OF SOLOMON

The purpose of this session is:

- To provide an overview of the themes of Job through the Song of Solomon;
- To discover how Jesus Christ is revealed in these books as God's Wisdom.

KEY VERSES

"I know that my Redeemer lives, and that in the end he will stand upon the earth. And after my skin has been destroyed, yet in my flesh I will see God; I myself will see him with my own eyes—I, and not another. How my heart yearns within me!" Job 19:25-27

"Praise the LORD. Sing to the LORD a new song, his praise in the assembly of the saints." Psalm 149:1

"Blessed is the man who finds wisdom, the man who gains understanding." Proverbs 3:13

"Fear God and keep his commandments, for this is the whole duty of man." Ecclesiastes 12:13

"He has taken me to the banquet hall, and his banner over me is love." Song of Solomon 2:4

Fold

"me" or "my," he or she is to substitute the word *"Jesus"* or *"Christ."* After they complete this responsive reading, discuss the following with the whole group:

Which parts of Proverbs 4 sound the most like Jesus' ministry? In what ways did Jesus embody Old Testament wisdom?

PURSUING GOD (5 MINUTES)

NEXT STEPS I NEED TO TAKE

- Ask the group members to remain in their pairs. Have each group member list the five qualities of wisdom on the hand-out that he or she needs in his or her own life.

- Once those qualities are listed, ask them to share those qualities with their partners and to prioritize them from the most to the least needed.

- Ask each group member to complete the following sentence for his or her partner:
  Jesus Christ is my wisdom when He _____ .

PRAYER (5 MINUTES)

PRAYING FOR WISDOM

- Have the whole group form a circle. Identify three areas in which they might pray for wisdom:
  In their families and/or marriages;
  In their church;
  In the country.

- Ask volunteers to say a sentence prayer for wisdom in one of these areas of life. As the leader, close the prayer time asking God to give each person God's wisdom.

SECTION ONE: GOD'S STORY (20 MINUTES)

THE WRITINGS: WISDOM AND SONGS FOR ALL OF LIFE

- Tell the group the Bible story doing the suggested activities as you come to them. Distribute the handout "Previewing God's Story in Job Through Song of Solomon" to group members.

OPTION ONE: (FOR A 90-MINUTE SESSION)

God Is My Strength and Refuge (15 Minutes)

- Explain to the group that real security comes from trusting God.
- Divide the whole group into six smaller groups. Assign the listed passages to each small group. Ask them to read their assigned passages and then write their completion for the following statement on their handouts:

  God is my refuge and strength when _____.

SECTION TWO: GOD'S PERSON (20 MINUTES)

THE BLESSED PERSON: ONE WHO IS WISE

- Explain that the person being studied is not a particular biblical character but the composite of a wise person in the Old Testament.
- Divide the whole group into four smaller groups, have each small group look up the assigned passages in the handout section "The Blessings of Wisdom" to discover how being wise in God will bless a believer.
- After 10 minutes, bring the whole group back together and discuss:

- - - - - - - - - - - - - - - - - Fold - - - - - - - - - - - - - - - - -

  What is required of the person who desires to be wise in the ways of God?
  What blessings are available to the righteous?
  The person wise in God's ways is _____.

- Complete the following one-sentence description:
  The person wise in God's ways is _____.

OPTION TWO: (FOR A 90-MINUTE SESSION)

Heart and Tongue Matters (15 Minutes)

- Explain to the group about the key themes of the heart and tongue in Proverbs.
- Divide the whole group into two groups—the "tongue group" and the "heart group." Each group scans Proverbs for passages on their topic having a recorder write down what they discover.
- Both groups come back together to share their discoveries and discuss:

  How are wise children of God supposed to guard their hearts?
  What should our tongues express?
  What should we keep from our tongues?

SECTION THREE: GOD'S SON (10 MINUTES)

JESUS CHRIST REVEALED AS GOD'S WISDOM

- Explain how Jesus is the Wisdom of God in the New Testament and read 1 Corinthians 1:24.
- Read John 1:1-5 to the group. Ask group members to find a partner. In each pair, ask that one partner read the odd-numbered verses and the other read the even-numbered verses of Proverbs 4 together. Each time the reader comes across the word "wisdom" or a personal pronoun like "I,"

PREVIEWING GOD'S STORY IN JOB
THROUGH SONG OF SOLOMON

1. God spoke to His people by revealing His wisdom and songs to Israel.

   Notes:

   Verses: Job 28:12-28; 38:36,37; Psalms 37:30,31; 51:6; 111:10; Proverbs 2:1-6; 4:5-12; 9:10; 24:3; Ecclesiastes 1:16-18; 7:11,12; 9:13-18; 10:12

   God's wisdom is...

   We are to acquire wisdom because...

2. In Hebrew the main word for God's wisdom is *chokmah* which means "wisdom, skill, willingness to be taught." It is the ability to apply God's will to specific situations.

   Notes:

3. Job's friends tried to interpret why he was suffering. Only God in His wisdom knew the whole picture.

   Notes:

CONTINUED

4. In the psalms, God is described in many ways: He is our Strength, Fortress and Rock who protects us (see Psalm 18); He is our loving Shepherd who guides us through life's difficulties even when present circumstances seem impossible (see Psalm 23).

Notes:

Verses: Psalms 3:1,2; 4:1; 6:3; 10:1; 13:1,2; 22:1; 24:3; 28:1; 38:1-4; 42:1,2; 43:1,2; 44:23-26; 51:10,11; 94:3; 102:1

5. In Proverbs, God desires for us to seek His wisdom and understanding. Repeatedly Proverbs declares that the fear—respect, awe and honor—of the Lord is the beginning of knowledge, understanding and wisdom.

Notes:

6. In Ecclesiastes, human wisdom and knowledge not centered in God is declared to be meaningless while true wisdom is to fear Him and keep His commandments (see Ecclesiastes 12:13,14).

Notes:

7. The Song of Solomon describes the wonderful and sometimes mysterious relationship of love between a husband and wife. This beautiful book has also been interpreted as describing the love relationship God has with His people (see Song of Solomon 1).

Notes:

CONTINUED

8. These books filled with the wisdom of God are called "the wisdom writings or wisdom literature." Remember this simple definition—true wisdom, knowledge and understanding is seeing life from God's perspective and not our own.

Notes:

THE BLESSINGS OF WISDOM

Group 1: Psalm 1

A. What is required of the person who is blessed?

B. What wise actions or attitudes are to be taken?

C. What are the blessings?

Group 2: Psalm 103

A. What is required of the person who is blessed?

CONTINUED

B. What wise actions or attitudes are to be taken?

C. What are the blessings?

Group 3: Proverbs 4

A. What is required of the person who is blessed?

B. What wise actions or attitudes are to be taken?

C. What are the blessings?

CONTINUED

Group 4: Ecclesiastes 7

A. What is required of the person who is blessed?

B. What wise actions or attitudes are to be taken?

C. What are the blessings?

Before next session, read:
Sunday: Satan and Saint (Job 1:1—2:13)
Monday: Bildad Thinks Job's a Hypocrite (Job 8:1-22)
Tuesday: Job Answers His Friends (Job 12:1-25)
Wednesday: Job's Faith (Job 19:1-29)
Thursday: Job and Elihu (Job 32:1-22; 37:23,24)
Friday: God Speaks to Job (Job 38:1-19)
Saturday: Job Vindicated and Honored (Job 42:1-17)

Understanding Job

The purpose of this session is:
- To provide an overview of the book of Job;
- To discover how Jesus Christ is revealed in Job as my Redeemer.

In this session, group members will learn:
- Key truths about God's story in Job;
- That Jesus Christ is revealed in the book of Job;
- The basic principle that God has a wise and eternal purpose for our suffering;
- How to apply these truths in Job to their own lives.

KEY VERSES

"Though [God] slay me, yet will I hope in him." Job 13:15

"I know that my Redeemer lives, and that in the end he will stand upon the earth. And after my skin has been destroyed, yet in my flesh I will see God; I myself will see him with my own eyes—I, and not another. How my heart yearns within me!" Job 19:25-27

"He knows the way that I take; when he has tested me, I will come forth as gold." Job 23:10

BEFORE THE SESSION

- Pray for group members by name, asking the Holy Spirit to teach the spiritual truths in Job to them.
- Read chapter 15 in *What the Bible Is All About*.
- Prepare copies of Session 2 handout "God's Story in Job" for group members.
- Check off these supplies once you have secured them:
    - ____ A chalkboard and chalk or a flip chart or an overhead projector with markers;
    - ____ Extra Bibles, pencils and paper for group members.
- If you are having a 90-minute session, carefully read the two option sections right now and pull together any supplies you need for them.

- Read the entire session and look up every passage. Have your Bible *Tuck-In*™ page ready for yourself.
- Arrive early and be ready to warmly greet each group member as he or she arrives.
- Memorize the key verses. Share them periodically and ask the group to repeat them as you teach the session.

SECTION ONE: GOD'S STORY (20 MINUTES)

JOB: TRIALS AND SUFFERING

Objective: To tell God's story in Job so that the group will understand the important truths about the purpose of suffering, testing and trials in the Christian life.

Greet everyone as they arrive. Before they are seated, ask them to greet four or five other people and complete the following sentence as they greet them:

One thing that I learned about Job in our preview session was _____.

Tell the following story, doing the suggested activities as you come to them. Distribute the handout "God's Story in Job" to group members.

Job is epic Hebrew poetry that reads like a narrative.

The book of Job opens with a scene in heaven and then tells of Job's fall from prosperity to poverty (see Job 1—2). In his misery, Job has a long discussion with four friends: Eliphaz, who is very sure of his theology; Bildad, who seeks to comfort with worn-out platitudes; Zophar, who presents himself as a wise, religious teacher; and Elihu, an impetuous youth.

Before looking specifically at these sections, write the following four categories on the board, flip chart or overhead:

(Eliphaz)	(Bildad)	(Zophar)	(Elihu)
Religious	Religious Cliché	Spiritual	Immature
Dogmatist	Person	Know-it-all	Believer

Ask: **What reason would each of these four friends give for Job's suffering in today's culture?** List the group member's responses under each heading.

Next, make a list of all the reasons that people without faith give to the question of why good people suffer. Do not yet begin to discuss the biblical answers for suffering.

The book of Job directly addresses the problem: Why do the righteous suffer?

One of the reasons for suffering is addressed in the first two chapters of the book: the great struggle between God and Satan. Sometimes people suffer because of Satan's attacks. In fact, Satan's attack on Job was based on his shallow view of Job's righteousness—that Job was godly for selfish reasons and that he served God for profit. Satan believed that when Job's prosperity ended, Job would curse God (see Job 1:1—2:8).

Ask the group to give examples of suffering that are caused by persecution of the righteous by either the world or the forces of evil.

Job's friends offer another reason for suffering: People suffer as a result of their own sins.

They reasoned that Job's great suffering was the result of great sin (see Job 4). While people do suffer and bring suffering on others because of their own mistakes and sin, the book of Job teaches that Job's suffering was not due to his sin.

With the whole group discuss the following questions:

How do we, at times, judge others because we believe they have brought the suffering on themselves? (For example, we believe all poor people suffer because they are unwilling to work or sick people suffer because they haven't taken care of themselves. In other words, sometimes we believe that those who suffer deserve to suffer.)

How can we avoid being judgmental toward suffering people?

How can we best minister to those who are suffering ?

Elihu offered yet another possible reason for suffering: Affliction is the chastisement of a loving Father and that suffering is sent to keep us from sinning further (see Job 36).

In fact, when God corrects us we may wrongly view that chastisement as suffering. However, this was not the case with Job.

Ask for any group members who would be willing to share a time when God was chastising or correcting them, and they thought it was suffering. As the leader you may have to share an example to encourage others to share.

Job questioned God. After revealing Himself to Job, God questioned him.

While questioning Job, God actually revealed one of the most important lessons about suffering: the godly are allowed to suffer so that they take a good honest look at themselves. Job was a good man, but he was self-righteous (see Job 38—41).

Have the group read Job 29:1-25. Give everyone about two minutes to circle and count in their Bibles the number of times that Job used "I," "my" or "me" in this passage. These personal pronouns are used 52 times in these verses. Job was self-centered. Have everyone turn to Job 38:1-7 and read it. Discuss the following as a group: **How does God begin to answer Job?**

Assign the following passages to be read aloud to the whole group: Genesis 17:1-3; Isaiah 6:1-5; Daniel 10:4-8; Romans 7:14-20. Discuss the following: **What do these passages teach us about self-righteousness and our inner struggles to resist sin?**

The book of Job reveals that God has a wise purpose for suffering.

Job was humbled and his self-righteousness was broken (see Job 42:4-6). Job lays the foundation for our understanding that God can bring redemptive good out of suffering just as He did through His own Son's suffering and death for us on the Cross.

Share the following redemptive purposes God has for our suffering:
1. **God wants to show His manifold wisdom through suffering** (see Ephesians 3:10).
2. **God wants the trial of our faith to work patience** (see Romans 5:5).
3. **God wants to refine the gold in our lives by fire** (see 1 Peter 1:7).
4. **God wants to reveal our real character that we might become like Christ** (see Philippians 3:10,11).

Ask everyone to find a partner and share which of the purposes they have experienced in their own lives and how they grew spiritually through the experience of suffering.

How little Job realized that so much hung on his steadfast trust in God when he said, "Though he slay me, yet will I hope in him" (Job 13:15).

Ask the group to mark the lines in their handouts concerning their own personal attitudes toward trials, tests and suffering in life. Then ask them to share their responses with their partners.

The book of Job does not answer all our questions about suffering, but it does reveal to us that only God fully understands or brings redemption through suffering. No human or religious explanation of suffering can comfort us apart

from the presence and comfort of a living God. Job's final comfort came only from God (see Job 19:25-27; 42:10).

With the whole group, ask group members to share some more comforting ways Job's friends might have ministered to him. Then ask for one or two testimonies on how God has comforted someone in a time of suffering even though he or she didn't have all the answers as to why they were suffering.

OPTION ONE: (FOR A 90-MINUTE SESSION)

"Spirit of the Living God" (15 Minutes)

Say: **There is a familiar chorus by Daniel Iverson titled "Spirit of the Living God."** If the group knows it, sing it through once. Otherwise share these words: **"Spirit of the living God, fall afresh on me; melt me; mold me; fill me, use me." This is what happened to Job. He experienced being broken and having God's Spirit deal with his life.**

Divide the group into three smaller groups. Assign the following verses to the groups:

Group One:	Job 16:12,14; 17:11
Group Two:	Job 23:10; 40:4
Group Three:	Job 19:21; 23:16; 42:3-6

Ask each group to list Job's different attitudes during his suffering. (Some of the attitudes they will find are: brokenness, being melted, repentance, being softened, receiving a touch from God, being humbled.) Then ask each group to report back to the whole group what they discovered.

Now have the whole group read Job 19:25,26. Discuss the following:

What kind of hope does Job have?

How does Job's hope give comfort to us? Have the group also read John 11:25.

Ask each person to find a partner and share their responses to the following:

The attitude I usually have when I suffer is _____.

If I were to sing "Spirit of the Living God," the part I need most is _____.

(Choose one and share why: "fall afresh on me," "melt me," "mold me," "fill me" or "use me.")

Section Two: God's Person (20 Minutes)

Job: Learning Through Suffering

Objective: To learn how perseverance and patience are developed through suffering and trials.

Have everyone read James 5:11. Ask the whole group to develop a definition of perseverance and patience. Write their definition on the board.

Ask everyone to find a partner and to explore the biblical definitions of patience and perseverance. The passages they are to explore together are found on their handout section "Perseverance and Suffering."

After about 15 minutes, discuss the following questions with the whole group:

How does our culture portray suffering?

What causes us to avoid suffering and trials?

Read this statement: **God is more concerned with our response to a circumstance than the circumstance itself.** Ask: **Do you agree or disagree, and why? How would you reword the statement to make it fit the book of Job?**

Option Two: (For a 90-Minute Session)

Satan and the Saint (15 Minutes)

One of the mysteries of Job is its treatment of Satan. Satan appears at the throne of God with the angelic beings (see Job 1:6).

With the whole group, brainstorm everything they know about Satan and write their observations on the board, flip chart or overhead.

To gain a clearer understanding of what Satan can and cannot do, divide the group into three groups to read the following passages and report what they have discovered about Satan:

Group One:	John 8:44; 10:10; 2 Corinthians 11:14
Group Two:	John 12:31; 16:11; Ephesians 2:2; 6:11
Group Three:	Matthew 4:1-11; Romans 16:20; James 4:7.

After the groups have read and reported to the whole group on their verses, discuss the following with the whole group:

While Satan can tempt and attack, what can Satan not do? Part of this discussion would include that Satan was only able to do what God permitted (see Job 1:10,12) and that we are never tempted beyond what we can endure (see 1 Corinthians 10:13).

When Satan attacked Job, how did Job respond? He did not blame God; he grieved (Job 1:20-22); he recognized that trials and tribulations are part of life; he cried out to God.

Have various group members read John 16:33; Romans 8:28 and James 1:12-18 out loud.

What do these passages tell us about experiencing life's difficulties and how God desires that we respond?

SECTION THREE: GOD'S SON (10 MINUTES)

JESUS CHRIST REVEALED AS MY REDEEMER

Objective: To discover how Jesus suffered and died to redeem us from sin.

Read Job 19:25-27 to the whole group. Say: **One of Job's greatest affirmations of faith is in Job 19:25-27. Even though he thinks the disease will kill him, the faith that he will see his Redeemer in the life to come is unshakable. How is Job's faith echoed in 1 John 3:2,3?**

Though Job suffered great loss and pain, his suffering pales in comparison to Jesus' suffering. Job was a righteous man (see Job 1:8), **but Jesus was perfectly innocent, and yet He was persecuted, rejected and crucified. How do Jesus' sufferings give us hope and comfort?**

Ask the group members to find the drawing of the cross on their handouts. After reading Isaiah 53 and 1 Peter 2:20-25, ask each person to write down what Jesus suffered for us. Ask each person to find a partner and share his or her responses to the following:

I thank God that Jesus suffered and died for me because _____.

Because Jesus suffered, I know that when I suffer _____.

PURSUING GOD (5 MINUTES)

NEXT STEPS I NEED TO TAKE

Objective: To take a realistic assessment of one's relationship with Jesus and how that relationship might grow closer in the coming week.

Job's character was tested and revealed by his suffering. What steps do you need to take as you grow in your understanding of and response to suffering?

With the same partner, have each person complete the "Ways I Need to Grow in My Response to Suffering" checklist on the handout. Ask everyone to share what they have checked with their partners.

PRAYER (5 MINUTES)

PRAYING TO BE A COMFORTER

Objective: To close the session with a deeper desire to comfort those who suffer.

Job's friends certainly did not comfort him in his suffering. Second Corinthians 1:3-7 tells us to comfort others as God comforts us.

Ask the pairs to pray for one another. Ask them to include the following in their prayers:

1. Pray for comfort for the partner whenever he or she faces temptations, trials and suffering;
2. Pray that God will use him or her to comfort others;
3. Thank Jesus for suffering for us on the cross.

Session 2 Bible *Tuck-In*™

UNDERSTANDING JOB

The purpose of this session is:
- To provide an overview of the book of Job;
- To discover how Jesus Christ is revealed in Job as my Redeemer.

KEY VERSES

"Though [God] slay me, yet will I hope in him." Job 13:15

"I know that my Redeemer lives, and that in the end he will stand upon the earth. And after my skin has been destroyed, yet in my flesh I will see God; I myself will see him with my own eyes—I, and not another. How my heart yearns within me!" Job 19:25-27

"He knows the way that I take; when he has tested me, I will come forth as gold." Job 23:10

SECTION ONE: GOD'S STORY (20 MINUTES)

JOB: TRIALS AND SUFFERING

- Tell the group the Bible story, doing the suggested activities as you come to them. Distribute the handout "God's Story in Job" to group members.

---

about experiencing life's difficulties and how God desires for us to respond?

SECTION THREE: GOD'S SON (10 MINUTES)

JESUS CHRIST REVEALED AS MY REDEEMER

- Ask the group members to find the drawing of the cross on their handouts. After reading Isaiah 53 and 1 Peter 2:20-25, ask each person to write down what Jesus suffered for us.

- Then ask each person to share his or her responses to the following with a partner:
I thank God that Jesus suffered and died for me because

Because Jesus suffered, when I suffer I know that _____.

PURSUING GOD

NEXT STEPS I NEED TO TAKE

- With the same partner, have each person complete the checklist in the handout. Ask them to share with their partners what they have checked.

PRAYER (5 MINUTES)

PRAYING TO BE A COMFORTER

- Ask the pairs to pray for one another. Ask them to include the following in their prayers:

1. Pray for comfort for your partner whenever he or she faces temptations, trials and suffering;
2. Pray that God will use that person to comfort others;
3. Thank Jesus for suffering for us on the cross.

OPTION ONE: (FOR A 90-MINUTE SESSION)

"Spirit of the Living God" (15 Minutes)

- Share the chorus "Spirit of the Living God."
- Divide the whole group into three groups. Assign the following verses: Group One: Job 16:12,14; 17:11; Group Two: Job 23:10; 40:4; Group Three: Job 19:21; 23:16; 42:3-6.
- Ask each group to list Job's different attitudes during his suffering and prepare to report back.
- Have the whole group read Job 19:25,26 and discuss:
  What kind of hope does Job have?
  How does Job's hope give comfort to us? Have the group also read John 11:25.
- In pairs share:
  The attitude I usually have when I suffer is _____.
  If I were to sing "Spirit of the Living God," the part I need most is _____.
  (Choose one and share why: "fall afresh on me," "melt me," "mold me," "fill me" or "use me.")

SECTION TWO: GOD'S PERSON (20 MINUTES)

JOB: LEARNING THROUGH SUFFERING

- Have everyone read James 5:11. Ask the whole group to develop a definition of perseverance and patience. Write their definitions on the board, flip chart or overhead.
- Ask everyone to find a partner and to explore the biblical definitions of patience and perseverance. The passages they are to explore together are found on their handout section "Perseverance and Suffering."
- After 15 minutes, discuss with the whole group:
  How does our culture portray suffering?
  What causes us to avoid suffering and trials?

---- Fold ----

- Read this statement: God is more concerned with our response to a circumstance than the circumstance itself.
  Ask: Do you agree or disagree and why? How would you reword the statement to make it fit the book of Job?

OPTION TWO: (FOR A 90-MINUTE SESSION)

Satan and the Saint (15 Minutes)

- Say: **One of the mysteries of Job is its treatment of Satan. Satan appears at the throne of God with the angelic beings** (see Job 1:6).
- With the whole group, brainstorm everything they know about Satan and write their observations on the board, flip chart or overhead.
- Divide the whole group into three groups to read the following passages and report what they have discovered about Satan:

  Group One: John 8:44; 10:10; 2 Corinthians 11:14
  Group Two: John 12:31; 16:11; Ephesians 2:2; 6:11
  Group Three: Matthew 4:1-11; Romans 16:20; James 4:7

- After the groups have reported, discuss:
  While Satan can tempt and attack, what can Satan not do?
  Part of this discussion would include that Satan was only able to do what God permitted (see Job 1:10,12) and that we are never tempted beyond what we can endure (1 Corinthians 10:13).
  When Satan attacked Job, how did Job respond? He did not blame God; he grieved; he recognized that trials and tribulations are part of life; he cried out to God (see Job 1:20-22).
- Have various group members read John 16:33, Romans 8:28 and James 1:12-18. Ask: **What do these passages tell us**

GOD'S STORY IN JOB

1. Job is epic Hebrew poetry that reads like a narrative.

   Notes:

2. The book of Job directly addresses the problem: Why do the righteous suffer?

   Notes:

3. Job's friends offer another reason for suffering: People suffer as a result of their own sins.

   Notes:

4. Elihu offered yet another possible reason for suffering: Affliction is the chastisement of a loving Father and that suffering is sent to keep us from sinning further.

   Notes:

5. Job questioned God. After revealing Himself to Job, God questioned him.

   Notes:

6. The book of Job reveals that God has a wise purpose for suffering.

   Notes:

7. How little Job realized that so much hung on his steadfast trust in God when he said, "Though he slay me, yet will I hope in him" (Job 13:15).

   Notes:

Put an X on the line that describes how you usually respond. (If a statement does not apply, do not mark it.)
When I undergo trials, tests and sufferings, I usually...

blame God.	blame others.	blame myself.
pray.	keep it to myself.	complain.
get angry.	get depressed.	look for the silver lining.
try to figure out why.	get confused.	try to discover what God's purpose might be.

List some other ways you might respond:

CONTINUED

PERSEVERANCE AND SUFFERING

How would you personally define patience and perseverance?

Read these passages about patience and perseverance. Jot down a summary of what each says.

Romans 2:6,7 _____

Romans 5:3-5: _____

2 Corinthians 6:4: _____

Colossians 1:10,11: _____

1 Timothy 6:11: _____

How should your definition of patience and perseverance change in light of these passages?

JESUS SUFFERED FOR ME

Inside this cross, write down all the ways that Isaiah 53 and 1 Peter 2:20-25 describe the sufferings of Jesus.

CONTINUED

WAYS I NEED TO GROW IN MY RESPONSE TO SUFFERING

Check any of the following that fit you:

____ Complain less.

____ Pray more.

____ Repent of suffering that I cause.

____ Take responsibility for personal sin and mistakes.

____ Resist Satan.

____ Put on God's armor.

____ Have more compassion for others who suffer.

____ Remember more how Jesus suffered for me.

____ Accept God's discipline and correction with joy, not seeing it as suffering.

____ Use what I have learned from suffering to help and encourage others.

____ Other: _____

Before next session, read:

Sunday: Psalms of Law (Psalms 1; 19)

Monday: Psalms of Creation (Psalms 29; 104)

Tuesday: Psalms of Judgment (Psalms 52—53)

Wednesday: Psalms of Christ (Psalms 22; 40—41)

Thursday: Psalms of Life (Psalms 3; 31)

Friday: Psalms of the Heart (Psalms 37; 42)

Saturday: Psalms of God (Psalms 90; 139)

Understanding Psalms

The purpose of this session is:

- To provide an overview of Psalms;
- To discover how Jesus Christ is revealed in Psalms as our All-in-All.

In this session, group members will learn:

- Key truths about God's story in Psalms;
- That Jesus Christ is revealed in Psalms;
- The basic principle that God is our Creator, Provider and Protector, and He alone is worthy of our worship and praise.
- How to apply the truths in Psalms to their own lives.

KEY VERSES

"Blessed is the man who does not walk in the counsel of the wicked or stand in the way of sinners or sit in the seat of mockers." Psalm 1:1

"My God, my God, why have you forsaken me? Why are you so far from saving me, so far from the words of my groaning? O my God, I cry out by day, but you do not answer, by night, and am not silent. Yet, you are enthroned as the Holy One; you are the praise of Israel." Psalm 22:1-3

"The LORD is my shepherd, I shall not be in want." Psalm 23:1

"Create in me a pure heart, O God, and renew a steadfast spirit within me." Psalm 51:10

"He who dwells in the shelter of the Most High will rest in the shadow of the Almighty." Psalm 91:1

"Praise the LORD, O my soul; all my inmost being, praise his holy name." Psalm 103:1

BEFORE THE SESSION

- Pray for group members by name, asking the Holy Spirit to teach the spiritual truths in Psalms to them.
- Read chapter 16 in *What the Bible Is All About*.
- Prepare copies of the Session 3 handout "God's Story in Psalms" for group member.

- Check off these supplies once you have secured them:
  - _____ A chalkboard and chalk or flip chart or an overhead projector with markers.
  - _____ Make a poster for each of the following worship themes and put them up all around the room. Have felt-tip pens for people to write on the posters. Label a poster for each one of the following themes:

    God's Goodness, Forgiveness and Mercy

    Crying Out to God

    Praise and Adoration of God

    Singing Unto God

    Living Righteously for God

    Seeking God's Justice and Deliverance from the Wicked

    Proclaiming the Mighty Acts of God

    Trust and Faith in God

    Confessing Sin and Weakness
  - _____ Extra Bibles, pencils and paper for group members.
- If you are having a 90-minute session, carefully read the two option sections right now and pull together any supplies you need for them.
- Read the entire session and look up every passage. Have your Bible *Tuck-In*™ page ready for yourself.
- Arrive early and be ready to warmly greet each group member as he or she arrives.
- Memorize the key verses. Share them periodically and ask the group to repeat them as you teach the session.

SECTION ONE: GOD'S STORY (20 MINUTES)

PSALMS: THE BOOK OF PRAISES

Objective: To tell God's story in Psalms so group members will understand the important truths about praise and worship.

Greet everyone as they arrive. Tell the following story, doing the suggested activities as you come to them. Distribute the handout "God's Story in Psalms" to group members.

Session
3

Psalms is the national hymnbook of Israel.

The Hebrew title of this book, *tehillim*, means "praise." The term "psalm" is from the Greek word for harp or other stringed instruments. There are 150 poems to be set to music for worship. Worship is the central theme of Psalms—magnifying and praising the Lord; exalting His attributes, His names, His Word and His goodness. Many of the psalms are supplications for help, acknowledging God's authority in all of human experience.

Ask each person to skim through a few psalms and find a verse on each one of these topics:

1. A verse that praises God;
2. A verse that seeks God or asks Him to do something;
3. A verse that lifts up a name or attribute of God.

Invite anyone who wishes to share a verse that he or she has found.

The book of Psalms is organized into five sections or books. This arrangement was probably the result of when each group of psalms was added to the collection. There is a great deal of similarity and overlap among the five books, but each also has some areas of emphasis which are worth noting.

A major theme of Psalms 1—41 is humanity.

The blessed man or human is described in Psalms 1 and 8. Psalms 2 and 14 describe man fallen from his high position and becoming God's enemy. Psalms 16—41 portray man's redemption and prophetically describe how Christ Jesus redeems and restores humanity. In this section, righteousness means living according to God's will.

Have everyone fill out the section of the handout entitled "Like a Tree." Then have them skim over the first 41 psalms and look for: **more instructions for righteous living, the end results of the wicked and the blessings of living for God.** Ask them to jot down on their "trees" any additional references they have found. Then discuss what they have discovered and written down.

In the second section, Psalms 42—72 describe Israel's relationship with God.

First she abandons God which results in her ruin and destruction. Then Psalms 50—60 proclaim that Israel's only hope of redemption is God, her Redeemer. Finally, Israel's redemption is revealed in Psalms 61—72.

Divide the whole group into three small groups. Assign each group the following psalms to survey:

Group One: Psalms 42—49—Israel's Ruin
Group Two: Psalms 50—60—Israel's Redeemer
Group Three: Psalms 61—72—Israel's Redemption

Ask each group to find one or two passages that illustrate the theme of that section. After a few minutes have all the groups report back and share the verses they have discovered. The rest of the group can jot down these references in their notes.

The sanctuary is described in Psalms 73—89.

The care, maintenance and building of God's house is described in almost every psalm of this section. The importance and joy of being in God's house is echoed in Psalm 84:10, "Better is one day in your courts than a thousand elsewhere; I would rather be a doorkeeper in the house of my God than dwell in the tents of the wicked."

Invite volunteers to complete the following sentence:
I would rather be worshiping in God's house than _____.

Psalms 90—106 extol God as the earth's Creator, our Provider and Protector.

These psalms describe Israel's wanderings in the wilderness. Inspiring verses of God as our refuge are found in Psalms 90—91. "He who dwells in the shelter of the Most High will rest in the shadow of the Almighty. I will say of the Lord, 'He is my refuge and my fortress, my God, in whom I trust'" (Psalm 91:1,2).

Ask everyone to find a partner. Have them read Psalms 90 and 91 together. Instruct them: **Choose one or two verses that are most meaningful and share those verses with your partner, explaining why you chose them.**

The book of Psalms concludes with praise of God and His Word (Psalms 107—150).

Psalm 107:20 begins this praise, "He sent forth his word and healed them; he rescued them from the grave." Psalm 119 uses the letters of the Hebrew alphabet as an acrostic poem to describe God's Word and our relationship to His Word with majesty and power. Psalm 150 concludes the book of Psalms ringing with praises to God with all the instruments and abilities of His worshipers.

OPTION ONE: (FOR A 90-MINUTE SESSION)

Praying the Psalms (15 Minutes)

Ask everyone in the group to stay with the partner they had earlier in the session.

Explain to the group that many of the psalms are prayers or could be prayed as prayers. Some examples are Psalms 23, 51 and 103.

Instruct them to do the following with their partners:

- **Read through all three psalms.**
- **Choose one of the psalms that you wish to pray together.**
- **Share a verse or two from that psalm that describes something that you desire to lift up to the Lord in prayer right now.**
- **Mention a person that you know who might need this psalm as a prayer for his or her life. Share a prayer need that person may have that the psalm brings to mind.**
- **Pray the psalm in unison.**
- **Then pray for the people you have mentioned. Lift up one or two verses from the psalm that you particularly wish to pray for that person.**

SECTION TWO: GOD'S PERSON (20 MINUTES)

DAVID: THE HEART OF A WORSHIPER

Objective: To learn how David worshiped and praised God.

So many themes of worship and praise are found in the psalms of David. His worship is a model and example for us in our worship of God.

Point out to the group that you have put up posters around the room with some of the elements and themes of worship on them. Ask everyone to find five psalms of David. They are then to read through those psalms and every place they see a theme of worship in a particular verse to go to the sheets on the wall and write that reference down.

Once they have completed surveying their own five psalms, encourage everyone to go around to each poster and write down the references for themselves for future reading and study about worship.

These are the poster themes:

    God's Goodness, Forgiveness and Mercy

    Crying Out to God

    Praise and Adoration of God

    Singing unto God

    Living Righteously for God

    Seeking God's Justice and Deliverance from the Wicked

Proclaiming the Mighty Acts of God

Trust and Faith in God

Confessing Sin and Weakness

With the whole group discuss:

How are some of these themes in our worship today?

How could we use the psalms more in our own devotional times and personal worship?

OPTION TWO: (FOR A 90-MINUTE SESSION)

Praising the Names and Nature of God in the Psalms (15 Minutes)

Divide the whole group into groups of four or five. Tell them that they will have five minutes to survey the book of Psalms. They are to assign one person as their recorder. The others in the group are to divide up the psalms among the persons in their group. Everyone is to survey their assigned psalms looking for names or attributes of God in those psalms. As they find one, they simply call out that name or attribute to their recorder.

After five minutes, ask the groups to stop and have the recorders slowly read back the list to their groups. Ask everyone in the small group to listen closely and to select their favorite name or attribute of God and to select one that is new or unfamiliar to them. Then have everyone share what they have selected and why.

After this sharing, come back together as a whole group and ask each person to complete this sentence:

I praise God that He is _____.

After each person has shared, read Psalm 150 in unison with feeling, praise and expression.

SECTION THREE: GOD'S SON (10 MINUTES)

JESUS CHRIST REVEALED AS OUR ALL-IN-ALL

Objective: To discover how Jesus is portrayed as our All-in-All in the psalms.

Refer the group members to their handouts. There is a matching exercise entitled "Jesus in Psalm 22" for them to see how the psalms prophetically reveal Jesus. They are to work on their matching exercises in pairs. The correct matching verses are:

> **Psalm 22:1 and Matthew 27:46;**
> **Psalm 22 6,7 and Luke 23:35,36;**
> **Psalm 22:8 and Matthew 27:43;**
> **Psalm 22:16 and John 19:18;**
> **Psalm 22: 18 and Luke 23:34;**
> **Psalm 22:28 and 1 Corinthians 15:23,24;**

After the pairs have completed their matching exercises, have the whole group discuss:

How did Jesus use the psalms in His own life?

What can we learn from Him for our own use of the psalms?

PURSUING GOD (5 MINUTES)

NEXT STEPS I NEED TO TAKE

Objective: To take a realistic assessment of one's relationship with Jesus and how that relationship might grow closer in the coming week.

In pairs, ask group members to read through Psalm 119 and find (write the following list on the board, flip chart or overhead):

* **One verse that tells them how important God's Word is;**
* **One action they need to take in applying God's Word in their own lives;**
* **One way they can get the Word of God into their hearts.**

PRAYER (5 MINUTES)

PRAYING PSALM 91

Objective: To close the session by praying through a psalm.

Explain to the group (especially if you have not done Option One) the importance of using the psalms in our prayer lives. Have everyone find a partner. Ask them to look up Psalm 91. Instruct each person to replace the personal pronouns in Psalm 91 with the name of his or her partner and pray that psalm aloud for him or her. As an example, say these verses for the group:

"John, who dwells in the shelter of the Most High will rest in the shadow of the Almighty" (v. 1).

"If John makes the Most High John's dwelling—even the Lord, who is John's refuge" (v. 9).

"John will call upon me, and I will answer John" (v. 15).

Close the group session in a circle of prayer. Pray Psalm 23 in unison as the closing prayer.

Session 3 Bible *Tuck-In*™

UNDERSTANDING PSALMS

The purpose of this session is:

- To provide an overview of Psalms;
- To discover how Jesus Christ is revealed in Psalms as our All-in-All.

KEY VERSES

"Blessed is the man who does not walk in the counsel of the wicked or stand in the way of sinners or sit in the seat of mockers." Psalm 1:1

"My God, my God, why have you forsaken me? Why are you so far from saving me, so far from the words of my groaning? O my God, I cry out by day, but you do not answer, by night, and am not silent. Yet, you are enthroned as the Holy One; you are the praise of Israel." Psalm 22:1-3

"The LORD is my shepherd, I shall not be in want." Psalm 23:1

"Create in me a pure heart, O God, and renew a steadfast spirit within me." Psalm 51:10

"He who dwells in the shelter of the Most High will rest in the shadow of the Almighty." Psalm 91:1

"Praise the LORD, O my soul; all my inmost being, praise his holy name." Psalm 103:1

SECTION THREE: GOD'S SON (10 MINUTES)

JESUS CHRIST REVEALED AS OUR ALL-IN-ALL

- Refer the group members to their handout section "Jesus in Psalm 22." They are to work on their matching exercises in pairs. After the pairs have completed their matching exercises, discuss with the whole group:

How did Jesus use the psalms in His own life?

What can we learn from Him for our own use of the psalms?

PURSUING GOD (5 MINUTES)

NEXT STEPS I NEED TO TAKE

- In pairs, read through Psalm 119 and find the following (write the following list on the board, flip chart or overhead):

One verse that tells them how important God's Word is;

One action they need to take in applying God's Word in their own lives;

One way they can get the Word of God into their hearts.

PRAYER (5 MINUTES)

PRAYING PSALM 91

- Explain to the group (especially if you have not done Option One) the importance of using the psalms in our prayer lives. Have everyone find a partner. Ask them to look up Psalm 91. Instruct each person to replace the personal pronouns in Psalm 91 with the name of his or her partner and pray that psalm aloud for him or her.
- Give examples from the psalm of how to do this.
- Close the group session in a circle of prayer. Pray Psalm 23 in unison as the closing prayer.

SECTION ONE: GOD'S STORY (20 MINUTES)

PSALMS: THE BOOK OF PRAISES

- Tell the group the Bible story in the Psalms, doing the suggested activities as you come to them. Distribute the handout "God's Story in Psalms" to group members.

OPTION ONE: (FOR A 90-MINUTE SESSION)

Praying the Psalms (15 Minutes)

- Explain to the group that many of the psalms are prayers or could be prayed as prayers. Some examples are Psalms 23, 51 and 103. In the same pairs instruct them to do the following with their partners:

  Read through all three psalms.

  Choose one of the psalms that you wish to pray together. Share a verse or two from that psalm that describes something that you desire to lift up to the Lord in prayer right now.

  Mention a person that you know who might need this psalm as a prayer for his or her life. Share a prayer need that person may have that the psalm brings to mind. Pray the psalm in unison. Then pray for the people you have mentioned. Lift up one or two verses from the psalm that you particularly wish to pray for that person.

SECTION TWO: GOD'S PERSON (20 MINUTES)

DAVID: THE HEART OF A WORSHIPER

- Point out the worship posters around the room. Ask everyone to find five psalms of David and to read through those psalms. Every place they see a theme of worship in a

particular verse, go to the wall posters and write that reference down.

- Upon completion encourage everyone to go around to each poster and write down the references for themselves for future reading and study about worship. Discuss:

  How are some of these themes in our worship today? How could we use the psalms more in our own devotional times and personal worship?

OPTION TWO: (FOR A 90-MINUTE SESSION)

Praising the Names and Nature of God in the Psalms (15 Minutes)

- Divide into groups of four. Tell them that they will have five minutes to survey the book of Psalms. They are to assign one person as their recorder. The others in the group are to divide up the psalms among themselves. Everyone is to survey their assigned psalms looking for names or attributes of God in those psalms. As they find one, they simply call out that name or attribute to their recorder.

- After five minutes, ask the groups to stop and have the recorders slowly read back the list to their groups. Ask everyone in the small group to listen closely and to select their favorite name or attribute of God and to select one that is new or unfamiliar to them. Then have everyone share what they have selected and why.

- As a whole group, ask each person to complete this sentence: **I praise God that He is** _____.

- After each person has shared, have the whole group read Psalm 150 in unison with feeling, praise and expression.

GOD'S STORY IN PSALMS

1. Psalms is the national hymnbook of Israel.

   Notes:

2. A major theme of Psalms 1—41 is humanity.

   Notes:

Psalm 1: "Like a Tree"
Instructions: Read Psalm 1. The blessed person is described.
- Outside of the tree, write the things the wicked do that the righteous person is not to do.
- In the soil, write the things that the blessed person is to do to feed the righteous life.
- In the branches and leaves, write the fruit of the blessed life—the results of living for God.

CONTINUED

3. In the second section, Psalms 42—72 describe Israel's relationship with God.
    Group One: Psalms 42—49—Israel's Ruin

    Group Two: Psalms 50—60—Israel's Redeemer

    Group Three: Psalms 61—72—Israel's Redemption

    Notes:

4. The sanctuary is described in Psalms 73—89.

    Notes:

5. Psalms 90—106 extol God as the earth's Creator, our Provider and Protector.

    Notes:

6. The book of Psalms concludes with praise of God and His Word. (Psalms 107—150).

    Notes:

CONTINUED

Jesus in Psalm 22

Match the passages in Psalm 22 with the Scripture about Jesus in the New Testament. Draw lines between the matching passages.

Psalm 22:1	Luke 23:35,36
Psalm 22:6,7	Luke 23:34
Psalm 22:8	Matthew 27:46
Psalm 22:16	1 Corinthians 15:23,24
Psalm 22:18	John 19:18
Psalm 22:28	Matthew 27:43

Before next session, read:

Sunday: Get Wisdom (Proverbs 1—4)

Monday: To Sons (Proverbs 5—7)

Tuesday: Good and Bad (Proverbs 15—17)

Wednesday: Wise Words (Proverbs 20; 22; 31)

Thursday: All Is Vanity (Ecclesiastes 1—3)

Friday: Only God Satisfies (Ecclesiastes 11—12)

Saturday: Joyful Communion (Song of Solomon 1:1-7; 2:1-7)

Understanding Proverbs, Ecclesiastes and Song of Solomon

The purpose of this session is:

- To provide an overview of Proverbs, Ecclesiastes and Song of Solomon;
- To discover how Jesus Christ is portrayed in these books as our Wisdom, the Purpose of all living, and the Lover of our souls.

In this session, group members will learn:

- Key truths about God's story in these three books;
- That Jesus Christ is revealed in Proverbs, Ecclesiastes and Song of Solomon;
- The basic principles of godly love, wisdom and righteous living;
- How to apply the truths taught in these books.

KEY VERSES

"The fear of the LORD is the beginning of knowledge, but fools despise wisdom and discipline." Proverbs 1:7

"For the LORD gives wisdom, and from his mouth come knowledge and understanding." Proverbs 2:6

"Above all else, guard your heart, for it is the wellspring of life." Proverbs 4:23

"There is a way that seems right to a man, but in the end it leads to death." Proverbs 14:12; 16:25

"'Meaningless! Meaningless!' says the Teacher. 'Utterly meaningless! Everything is meaningless!'" Ecclesiastes 1:2

"Now all has been heard; here is the conclusion of the matter: Fear God and keep his commandments, for this is the whole duty of man." Ecclesiastes 12:13

"He has taken me to the banquet hall, and his banner over me is love." Song of Solomon 2:4

BEFORE THE SESSION

- Pray for group members by name, asking the Holy Spirit to teach the spiritual truths in these books to them.
- Read chapter 17 in *What the Bible Is All About*.
- Prepare copies of Session 4 handout, "God's Story in Proverbs, Ecclesiastes and Song of Solomon," for group members.
- Check off the following supplies once you have secured them:
    - ____ A chalkboard and chalk or a flip chart or an overhead projector with markers.
    - ____ Extra Bibles, pencils and paper for group members.
    - ____ 3x5-inch index cards, one for each group member.
- If you are having a 90-minute session, carefully read the two option sections right now and pull together any supplies you need for them.
- Read the entire session and look up every passage. Have your Bible *Tuck-In*™ page ready for yourself.
- Arrive early and be ready to warmly greet each group member as he or she arrives.
- Memorize the key verses. Share them periodically and ask the group to repeat them as you teach the session.

SECTION ONE: GOD'S STORY (20 MINUTES)

GOD'S STORY IN PROVERBS, ECCLESIASTES AND SONG OF SOLOMON

Objective: To tell God's story in these books so that Christians will apply the truths for wise living, understanding God's love for them and for their relationships with Him and one another.

Greet everyone as they arrive. Tell the following story, doing the suggested activities as you come to them. Distribute the handout "God's Story in Proverbs, Ecclesiastes and Song of Solomon" to group members.

In Proverbs, God provides practical wisdom for ordering our Christian lives.

- **In Psalms we find the Christian on his knees** (see Psalms 95:6); **in Proverbs, on his feet** (see Proverbs 4:26).
- **Psalms is for the Christian's devotions** (see Psalms 37); **Proverbs is for his walk** (see Proverbs 4).
- **Psalms is for the closet of prayer** (see Psalms 51); **Proverbs is for the business place, home and playground** (see Proverbs 31:10-31).

With the whole group, discuss:

How do the psalms help a Christian in his or her devotional life?

God's counsel of wisdom found in Proverbs may be divided into the following three sections:

- **Counsel for young people (chapters 1—10);**
- **Counsel for all men and women (chapters 11—20);**
- **Counsel for kings and rulers (chapters 21—31).**

Ask the group to recall the discussion about wisdom from the first session in this series. Put the word "wisdom" on the board and write down all the definitions that group members give to complete the following sentence:

God's wisdom is _____.

God counsels young people to "Wise Up!" "Walk Straight!" and "Watch Your Step!"

Young people are warned about God's "hit list" of behaviors to avoid—pride, lies, murder, deceit, mischief, betrayal and discord. He also warns them about the deceitful character of a foolish person, where to find true riches, and the misuse of the tongue (see Proverbs 2).

Assign each person in the group to read a few verses from Proverbs 2 and to look for the three most important pieces of wise advice for young people in their assigned verses. Then with the whole group, list the wise counsel for young people found in Proverbs 2.

God counsels all men and women about selfishness, foolishness, lying, dealing with anger, true friendship, and drinking (Proverbs 11—20). Guidance on parenting and timely advice on marriage are also found in Proverbs.

Assign everyone in the group at least one chapter from Proverbs 11—20 to skim over and find a favorite meaningful verse in his or her assigned chapter. After a few minutes, invite each person to read his or her favorite verse to the rest of the group.

God counsels kings and rulers—the leaders among us—to have self-control, a good reputation, sober judgment, godly marriages, understanding and just hearts, and to have security only in the Lord.

Proverbs 31 is the classic description of a godly woman.

Ask everyone to find one verse in Proverbs 22 that emphasizes the importance of self-control—one that can be applied to his or her life. Find a partner and share that verse with the partner. Have the partners pray for one another for self-control in that area of their lives.

For the Christian who explores Proverbs, Jesus is the beginning of all wisdom. In Ecclesiastes, the Christian can see that He is the end and purpose of all life.

In Proverbs, wisdom is seeing God's perspective and knowing Him. In Ecclesiastes, wisdom is prudence and discernment in what's truly meaningful in life. The key word in Ecclesiastes is "vanity" or "meaningless" (see Ecclesiastes 1:2).

Put the following list up on the board, flip chart or overhead.

Human Wisdom and Knowledge

Work

Seasons of Life

Friends

Success

Wealth and Prosperity

Education

Family

Pleasure

Philosophy and Religion

Say to the group: **All of these listed items are mentioned in Ecclesiastes as those things that people pursue in their lives. The final judgment is that all are meaningless without God being the purpose and end of all pursuits.** With the whole group, rank the order of the most important to the least important pursuits in the lives of most people in the community or nation.

Then discuss the following questions:

How does a relationship with God in Jesus Christ give meaning to these things? Read Matthew 5:19-34. In what ways does Jesus emphasize what Ecclesiastes says?

God reveals in Ecclesiastes the record of all that human thinking and natural religion has ever been able to discover. God through Solomon declares that our ways and pursuits are meaningless. All that ultimately matters is fearing, obeying and knowing God.

With the whole group, come to a consensus on the best way to complete the sentence:

The "fear of the Lord" means _____.

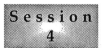

Now discuss the following:

What are the best ways that Christians can teach children what's really meaningful in life?

How can we communicate the fear of God in the proper perspective to our children?

God demonstrates the deep meaning of love in Song of Solomon. Cast in oriental language and imagery, this song of love in marriage portrays the kind of love that God has for His people and that Christ has for the Church.

Ask group members to take three minutes to skim through Song of Solomon and make a list of every quality of love they find in the book. Then list the qualities on the board, flip chart or overhead. Discuss the following:

What quality of God's love do we need most as the Church? As individual Christians?

What does Song of Solomon show us about marital love?

(**Note:** If you are doing Option One, leave this list on the board.)

OPTION ONE: (FOR A 90-MINUTE SESSION)

God's Love (15 Minutes)

Have group members form groups of four. In those small groups, ask them to read 1 Corinthians 13; Ephesians 5:22-32 and 1 John 4:7-21. Ask them to list on their handouts the godly qualities of love that they see in these passages.

After the small groups have completed their lists, ask them to compare these lists from the New Testament with the previously made list of qualities from Song of Solomon. With the whole group discuss:

How is the love described in Song of Solomon similar to that described in the New Testament?

Which qualities of love are most needed in marriages today? Why?

SECTION TWO: GOD'S PERSON (20 MINUTES)

GODLY MEN AND WOMEN: WISE IN THE LORD

Objective: To learn the marks of wise and godly men and women found in Proverbs.

Divide the whole group into one group of men and one group of women. If the class is large, subdivide the gender groups into smaller groups of five or six. Assign Proverbs 2 to the men and Proverbs 31 to the women. Ask each group to develop a list of godly attributes for their respective gender. Once the lists have been developed, ask the men and women to find a partner within their own gender group and share their responses to the following:

Which quality do I need most in my life?

Which quality is strongest in my life?

Then bring the whole group together. Have them share their lists. Write the lists on the board, flip chart or overhead, then discuss:

Which quality is most needed by men today in the Body of Christ?

Which quality is most needed by women today in the Body of Christ?

What can be done by the church to cultivate these qualities in men and women?

OPTION TWO: (FOR A 90-MINUTE SESSION)

Wisdom in Proverbs (15 Minutes)

Divide the group into six smaller groups. Assign each of the small groups one of the following topics. Tell them that their task is to survey the books of Proverbs and Ecclesiastes for wisdom on their assigned topic. They are to summarize that wisdom and make a short presentation to the whole group summarizing God's wisdom on that aspect of life.

Group One:	Wisdom, Knowledge and Fear of God
Group Two:	The Heart
Group Three:	The Tongue and Speech
Group Four:	Prosperity, Health and Blessing
Group Five:	Marriage
Group Six:	Parenting and Discipline

After all the groups have had five to seven minutes to survey these two books for their topic, then have each group report its summary to the rest of the groups. As time permits, have anyone who wishes share their completion to the following sentence:

The wisest advice that I have heard is _____.

SECTION THREE: GOD'S SON (10 MINUTES)

JESUS CHRIST REVEALED AS OUR WISDOM, THE PURPOSE OF LIFE AND THE LOVER OF OUR SOULS

Objective: To discover how Jesus embodies the qualities of wisdom described in Proverbs, Ecclesiastes and Song of Solomon.

Say to the group: **Jesus is the perfect embodiment of the wisdom we see in Proverbs, of the purpose of life in Ecclesiastes and of love in Song of Solomon.**

Assign three group members to read the following Scriptures to the group: 1 Corinthians 1:20-31; John 1:4 and 14:6; John 15:12-17.

Ask everyone to find a partner. Invite each pair to complete the sentences on their handouts under the section entitled, "Jesus: Our Wisdom, the Purpose of Life and the Lover of Our Souls."

Invite some of the pairs to share with the whole group how they have completed their sentences.

PURSUING GOD (5 MINUTES)

NEXT STEPS I NEED TO TAKE

Objective: To make a realistic assessment of one's relationship with Jesus and how that relationship might grow closer in the coming week.

In the same pairs share with one another from the section entitled "Ways I Need to Grow in Wisdom and Love" in the handout for this session. After sharing is completed, have the pairs pray for one another to be empowered by God in that area of growth.

PRAYER (5 MINUTES)

Objective: To close the session by praying through a psalm.

Give everyone in the group a 3x5-inch card. Ask everyone to write "Wisdom," "Life" and "Love" down the side of his or her card leaving space between each word for a sentence. Invite them to write a sentence prayer to God for each one of these words based on what they have learned from the books of Proverbs, Ecclesiastes and Song of Solomon.

Session 4 Bible *Tuck-In*™

UNDERSTANDING PROVERBS, ECCLESIASTES AND SONG OF SOLOMON

The purpose of this session is:

- To provide an overview of Proverbs, Ecclesiastes and Song of Solomon;
- To discover how Jesus Christ is portrayed as our Wisdom, the Purpose of all living, the Lover of our souls.

KEY VERSES

"The fear of the LORD is the beginning of knowledge, but fools despise wisdom and discipline." Proverbs 1:7

"For the LORD gives wisdom, and from his mouth come knowledge and understanding." Proverbs 2:6

"Above all else, guard your heart, for it is the wellspring of life." Proverbs 4:23

"There is a way that seems right to a man, but in the end it leads to death." Proverbs 14:12; 16:25

"'Meaningless! Meaningless!' says the Teacher. 'Utterly meaningless! Everything is meaningless!'" Ecclesiastes 1:2

"Now all has been heard; here is the conclusion of the matter: Fear God and keep his commandments, for this is the

---- Fold ----

69

---

mits, have anyone who wishes share their completion to the following sentence:

The wisest advice that I have heard is _____ .

SECTION THREE: GOD'S SON (10 MINUTES)

JESUS CHRIST REVEALED AS OUR WISDOM, THE PURPOSE OF LIFE AND THE LOVER OF OUR SOULS

- Assign three group members to read the following Scriptures to the rest of the group: 1 Corinthians 1:20-31; John 1:4 and 14:6; John 15:12-17.

- Ask everyone to find a partner. Ask each pair to complete the sentences on their handouts under the section entitled, "Jesus: Our Wisdom, the Purpose of Life and the Lover of Our Souls."

- Invite some of the pairs to share with the whole group how they have completed their sentences.

PURSUING GOD (5 MINUTES)

NEXT STEPS I NEED TO TAKE

- In the same pairs share with one another from the section entitled "Ways I Need to Grow in Wisdom and Love" on the handout for this session. After sharing, have them pray for one another to be empowered by God in that area of growth.

PRAYER (5 MINUTES)

- Give everyone a 3x5-inch card. Ask everyone to write "Wisdom," "Life" and "Love" down the side of his or her card leaving space between the words for a short sentence. Invite them to write a sentence prayer to God for each one of these words based on what they have learned from the books of Proverbs, Ecclesiastes and Song of Solomon.

whole duty of man." Ecclesiastes 12:13

"He has taken me to the banquet hall, and his banner over me is love." Song of Solomon 2:4

SECTION ONE: GOD'S STORY (20 MINUTES)

GOD'S STORY IN PROVERBS, ECCLESIASTES AND SONG OF SOLOMON

• Greet everyone as they arrive. Tell the group the story, doing the suggested activities as you come to them. Distribute the handout "God's Story in Proverbs, Ecclesiastes and Song of Solomon" to group members.

OPTION ONE: (FOR A 90-MINUTE SESSION)

God's Love (15 Minutes)

• Have group members form groups of four. In those small groups, ask them to read 1 Corinthians 13; Ephesians 5:22-32 and 1 John 4:7-21. Ask them to list on their handouts the godly qualities of love that they see in these passages. After the small groups have completed and compared their lists, discuss with the whole group:

How is the love described in Song of Solomon similar to that described in the New Testament?
Which qualities of love are most needed in marriages today? Why?

SECTION TWO: GOD'S PERSON (20 MINUTES)

GODLY MEN AND WOMEN: WISE IN THE LORD

• Divide the whole group into one group of men and one group of women. If class is large, subdivide the gender

groups into smaller groups of five or six. Assign Proverbs 2 to the men and Proverbs 31 to the women. Ask each group to develop a list of godly attributes for their respective genders. Once the lists have been developed, ask the men and women to find a partner within their gender group and share their responses to the following:

Which quality do I need most in my life?
Which quality is strongest in my life?

• Then bring the whole group together. Have them share their lists. As they share, write the lists on the board, flip chart or overhead. Discuss:

Which quality is most needed by men today in the Body of Christ?
Which quality is most needed by women today in the Body of Christ?
What can be done by the Church to cultivate these qualities in men and women?

OPTION TWO: (FOR A 90-MINUTE SESSION)

Wisdom in Proverbs (15 Minutes)

• Divide the group into six smaller groups. Assign each of the small groups one of the topics. Tell them that their task is to survey the books of Proverbs and Ecclesiastes for wisdom on their subject. They are to summarize their findings and make a short presentation to the whole group summarizing God's wisdom on that area of life.

• After all the groups have had five to seven minutes to survey these two books for their topic, then have each group report its summary to the rest of the groups. As time per-

GOD'S STORY IN PROVERBS,
ECCLESIASTES AND SONG OF SOLOMON

1. In Proverbs, God provides practical wisdom for ordering our Christian lives.

   Notes:

2. God counsels young people to "Wise Up!" "Walk Straight!" and "Watch Your Step!"

   Notes:

3. God counsels all men and women about selfishness, foolishness, lying, dealing with anger, true friendship and drinking (Proverbs 11—20). Guidance on parenting and timely advice on marriage are also found in Proverbs.

   Notes:

4. God counsels kings and rulers—the leaders among us—to have self-control, a good reputation, sober judgment, godly marriages, understanding and just hearts, and to have security only in the Lord.

   Notes:

5. For the Christian who explores Proverbs, Jesus is the beginning of all wisdom. In Ecclesiastes, the Christian can see that He is the end and purpose of all life.

> Human Wisdom and Knowledge
> Work
> Seasons of Life
> Friends
> Success
> Wealth and Prosperity
> Education
> Family
> Pleasure
> Philosophy and Religion

Notes:

6. God reveals in Ecclesiastes the record of all that human thinking and natural religion has ever been able to discover. God through Solomon declares that our ways and pursuits are meaningless. All that ultimately matters is fearing, obeying and knowing God.

Notes:

7. God demonstrates the deep meaning of love in Song of Solomon. Cast in oriental language and imagery, this song of love in marriage portrays the kind of love that God has for His people and that Christ has for the Church.

Notes:

CONTINUED

GOD'S LOVE IN...

1 Corinthians 13	Ephesians 5:22-32	1 John 4:7-21	Song of Solomon
_____	_____	_____	_____
_____	_____	_____	_____
_____	_____	_____	_____
_____	_____	_____	_____
_____	_____	_____	_____
_____	_____	_____	_____

JESUS: OUR WISDOM, THE PURPOSE OF LIFE AND THE LOVER OF OUR SOULS

After surveying these books, complete these sentences:

In Proverbs, wisdom is...

Jesus fulfills wisdom in that He...

In Ecclesiastes, the end or purpose of life is...

CONTINUED

Jesus is the end or purpose of life in that He...

In the Song of Solomon, love is...

Jesus is love in that He...

WAYS I NEED TO GROW IN WISDOM AND LOVE

Underline the areas of your life that need deeper wisdom from God. Circle the areas that need deeper love from God. You may both underline and circle certain items as they require both deeper love and wisdom.

> My finances.
> Relationship with a spouse.
> Relationship with a child.
> Relationship with another family.
> Relationships at work.
> Family relationships.
> Solving a major crisis.
> God's will for my future.
> Knowing how to make a major decision in my life.

CONTINUED

Before the next session, read:

Monday: The Calling of the Prophets (Isaiah 6; Jeremiah 1; Jonah 1)

Tuesday: God Speaking Judgment Through His Prophets (Hosea 4; Amos 5; Malachi 3)

Wednesday: The Prophetic Day of the Lord (Joel 2; Zephaniah 1; Malachi 4)

Thursday: The New Covenant (Isaiah 43; Ezekiel 18; Jeremiah 31)

Friday: The Exile and Restoration (Jeremiah 3; Ezekiel 7; Daniel 1; Hosea 14)

Saturday: The Coming Messiah (Isaiah 9; 53; Micah 5:1-5; Zechariah 14)

Previewing the Prophets: Isaiah Through Malachi

The purpose of this session is:

- To provide an overview of the prophets;
- To discover how Jesus Christ is revealed as the Fulfillment of prophecy.

In this session, group members will learn:

- Key truths about God's story in the prophetic books;
- That Jesus Christ is revealed in the prophets.
- The basic principles and major themes of prophetic revelation;
- How to apply the basic truths from the prophets to their own lives.

KEY VERSES

"Yet the LORD testified against Israel, and against Judah, by all the prophets, and by all the seers, saying, 'Turn ye from your evil ways, and keep my commandments and my statutes, according to all the law which I commanded your fathers, and which I sent to you by my servants the prophets.'" 2 Kings 17:13, *KJV*

"In the past God spoke to our forefathers through the prophets at many times and in various ways." Hebrews 1:1

BEFORE THE SESSION

- Pray for group members by name, asking the Holy Spirit to teach the spiritual truths of these books to them.
- Read chapter 26 and skim chapters 18 through 25 in *What the Bible Is All About*.
- Prepare copies of Session 5 handouts "God's Story in the Prophets" and "Times of the Prophets."
- Check off the following supplies once you have secured them:
  - _____ A chalkboard and chalk or a flip chart or an overhead projector with markers;
  - _____ Extra Bibles, pencils and paper for group members;
  - _____ Strong's, Young's or Cruden's Concordance.

- If you are having a 90-minute session, carefully read the two option sections right now and pull together any supplies you need for them.
- Read the entire session and look up every passage. Have your Bible *Tuck-In*™ page ready for yourself.
- Arrive early and be ready to warmly greet each group member as he or she arrives.
- Memorize the key verses. Share them periodically as you teach the session and ask the group to repeat them.

SECTION ONE: GOD'S STORY (20 MINUTES)

GOD'S STORY IN THE PROPHETS

Objective: To tell God's story in these books so that Christians will apply the truths from the prophets to their own lives.

Greet everyone as they arrive. Tell the following story, doing the suggested activities as you come to them. Distribute the handout "God's Story in the Prophets" to group members.

What is a *nabi*? A *nabi* is a prophet. So, what is a prophet?

Go over to one person in the room and whisper: **God says, "Be just in all your courts."** Now tell that to the group. Go to another person and whisper: **God says, "Be righteous in all your relationships."** Now tell that to the group. After these people have repeated their sentences, proceed with your story.

A prophet is God's mouthpiece. A prophet speaks God's Word to His people.

That word may be encouraging or judging, uplifting or seeking repentance (see Isaiah 6:8-10).

Ask the group: **When you hear the word "prophet," what immediately comes to your mind?** As group members call out what comes to mind, write their responses on the board, flip chart or overhead. Ask group members to agree on one or two items on the board that best define what they believe a prophet to be.

A popular notion about prophets is that they primarily foretell the future. Actually, a better way to describe prophets is that they walk with God so closely that God reveals to them what He is about to do.

Prophets boldly "forthtell" God's Word about both the present and the future.

Chronologically, the prophets can be divided into three periods: pre-exile, exile and post-exile (i.e. before, during or after the exile). The books of the prophets are divided into the major prophets—Isaiah, Jeremiah and Lamentations, Ezekiel and Daniel—and the minor prophets which are all the remaining books of the Old Testament. Major prophets simply means that their books are longer than the books of the minor prophets.

Divide the whole group into two groups. Assign one group to look through Isaiah. Assign the other group to look through Jeremiah. Ask both groups to find two prophecies that relate to their prophet's present day and two prophecies that relate to the future.

Give everyone in the group the Session 5 handout "Times of the Prophets." Have everyone identify where various prophets are found in history. Find the pre-exile, exile and post-exile prophets.

Certain major themes dominate most of the prophets.

Those themes include repentance, God's judgment and wrath (see Amos 5:18-22), God's desire to forgive and restore (see Hosea 14:1-9) and the coming Messiah bringing righteousness and justice in society (see Isaiah 9:2-7).

Assign either Amos 5, Hosea 14 or Isaiah 9 to each group. Ask each group to find a verse or short passage in their assigned chapters that would illustrate one of the corresponding themes listed above.

The prophetic books point to the coming kingdom of God established by the Messiah.

Messiah means "anointed one." The Anointed One of God would have the qualities of a king, a priest and a prophet.

Assign the following passages to various group members to read out loud so that they can hear examples of some of the Messianic prophecies:

Isaiah 9:6,7; 32:1-3; 42:1-4; 53:1-10;
Jeremiah 23:5;
Daniel 2:44, 7:13,14;
Micah 5:2;
Zechariah 11:12;
Malachi 3:1.

OPTION ONE: (FOR A 90-MINUTE SESSION)

Prophets: Messengers for Their Day and Ours (15 Minutes)

Divide the whole group into three groups. Assign each small group one of the themes in the prophets. When they skim their prophet's book and have found examples of their themes, they are to paraphrase the verses. After about seven minutes of searching out the verses, they are to write a one-paragraph summary statement of these verses. That summary statement should be in contemporary language as if the prophets were addressing our generation.

> Group One—God's Justice, Judgment and Wrath: Amos 5:21-23 and Hosea 4:5-9
>
> Group Two—God Will Redeem His People: Joel 2:25-27, Zechariah 14:9-11 and Zephaniah 3:14-20
>
> Group Three—God's Future Judgment of History: Ezekiel 36:26-28 and Daniel 7:9-14

After the small groups have written their summaries, have them share their summaries with the whole group.

SECTION TWO: GOD'S PERSON (20 MINUTES)

ELIJAH AND ELISHA: BOLD PROPHETS OF GOD

Objective: To look at these two prophets as examples of Old Testament prophets.

Divide the whole group into two groups. Tell each small group that they are to choose three scenes from the life of each prophet and to act out or role-play those scenes for the other group. The actors can recite their lines or a narrative can be read while group members act out the story or the group may decide to mime the story and see if those watching can guess the story.

Group One: Elijah—1 Kings 17—19.
Group Two: Elisha—2 Kings 1—6.

After both groups have presented their dramas or mimes, discuss the following:

What godly qualities do you see in both prophets' lives?

How would people today respond to such prophetic qualities in people?

After this discussion, put the following list on the board, flip chart or overhead:

> **The prophets had a message directly from God...**
>
> 1. **For their own time and people.**
> 2. **For future events related to God's people, the Messiah and the kingdom that God would establish for His people in the future.**
> 3. **For us today to apply to our own lives.**

Ask each person in the group to choose one of these three aspects of prophetic messages. Invite them to share with the whole group an example that they have seen in the prophets of the type of message that they selected.

OPTION TWO: (FOR A 90-MINUTE SESSION)

The Character of the Prophets (15 Minutes)

Say to the group: **The prophets boldly exposed sin, injustice, rebellion and formalized religion in their day. What were the prophets really like?**

Ask everyone in the group to choose one prophet. Tell them to spend five minutes skimming their prophet's book and answering the following three questions: (Write the questions on the board, flip chart or overhead to remind them what to look for as they are surveying their books.)

What clues does this book give us about the prophet's character?

What is the main theme of this prophet's message?

How would this prophet be received today by the Church?

After everyone has had the time to survey the books, invite everyone to share about their particular prophet.

SECTION THREE: GOD'S SON (10 MINUTES)

JESUS CHRIST REVEALED AS THE FULFILLMENT OF PROPHECY
Objective: To discover how Jesus embodies the qualities of God's ultimate, prophetic Messenger to humanity.

Divide the class into two groups. Give each group a large piece of newsprint or poster board and a felt-tip pen. The first group is to turn to Isaiah 53 and list every quality about Jesus' life that they find. The second group is to use the concordance and list every verse in the Gospel of Matthew in which Jesus refers to the words "prophet," "prophets," "prophecy" or "prophesy." Then with the whole group discuss:

How did Jesus fulfill the prophecy in Isaiah 53 through His death?
What did Jesus say about fulfilling the prophecies and how He would be received like the prophets of old?

PURSUING GOD (5 MINUTES)

NEXT STEPS I NEED TO TAKE
Objective: To make a realistic assessment of one's relationship with Jesus and how that relationship might grow closer in the coming week.

Have everyone find a partner. Say: **Share with your partner one way that God has called you to speak His word to your spouse, family or friends. After you share, pray that the Lord will give each of you the courage to speak His Word as He leads you.**

PRAYER (5 MINUTES)

Objective: To seek to hear God's voice through the prophets.

Ask each person to sit alone and read Jonah 2:2-9 as a personal prayer. Suggest that they select one verse from the prayer and say it out loud as a prayer to God.

Have the whole group form a circle. Ask volunteers to share a verse from Jonah's prayer that is particularly meaningful to them. Then close the session with a prayer thanking God for His salvation.

Session 5 Bible *Tuck-In*™

PREVIEWING THE PROPHETS: ISAIAH THROUGH MALACHI

The purpose of this session is:
- To provide an overview of the prophets;
- To discover how Jesus Christ is revealed as the Fulfillment of prophecy.

KEY VERSES

"Yet the LORD testified against Israel, and against Judah, by all the prophets, and by all the seers, saying, 'Turn ye from your evil ways, and keep my commandments and my statutes, according to all the law which I commanded your fathers, and which I sent to you by my servants the prophets." 2 Kings 17:13, KJV

"In the past God spoke to our forefathers through the prophets at many times and in various ways." Hebrews 1:1

SECTION ONE: GOD'S STORY IN THE PROPHETS

GOD'S STORY IN THE PROPHETS

- Greet everyone as they arrive. Tell the group the Bible story, doing the suggested activities as you come to them.

"prophets," "prophecy" or "prophesy." Then with the whole group discuss:

How did Jesus fulfill the prophecy in Isaiah 53 through His death?

What did Jesus say about fulfilling the prophecies and how He would be received like the prophets of old?

PURSUING GOD (5 MINUTES)

NEXT STEPS I NEED TO TAKE

- Have everyone find a partner. Say: Share with your partner one way that God has called you to speak His word to your spouse, family or friends. After you share, pray that the Lord will give each of you the courage to speak His Word as He leads you.

PRAYER (5 MINUTES)

- Ask each person to sit alone and read Jonah 2:2-9 as a personal prayer. Suggest that they select one verse from the prayer and say it out loud as a prayer to God.
- Have the whole group form a circle. Ask volunteers to share a verse from Jonah's prayer that is particularly meaningful to them. Then close the session with a prayer thanking God for His salvation.

Distribute the handout "God's Story in the Prophets" to group members.

OPTION ONE: (FOR A 90-MINUTE SESSION)

Prophets: Messengers for Their Day and Ours (15 Minutes)

• Divide the whole group into three groups. Assign each small group one of the themes in the prophets. When they skim their prophet's book and have found examples of their themes, they are to paraphrase the verses. After about seven minutes of searching out the verses, they are to write a one-paragraph summary statement of these verses. That summary statement should be in contemporary language as if the prophets were addressing our generation. Have them share their summaries with the whole group.

Group One—God's Justice, Judgment and Wrath: Amos 5:21-23 and Hosea 4:5-9

Group Two—God Will Redeem His People: Joel 2:25-27; Zechariah 14:9-11 and Zephaniah 3:14-20

Group Three—God's Future Judgment of History: Ezekiel 36:26-28 and Daniel 7:9-14

SECTION TWO: GOD'S PERSON (20 MINUTES)

ELIJAH AND ELISHA: PROPHETS OF GOD

• Divide the whole group into two groups. Using drama or mime, have each group act out three stories from that prophet's life.

    Group One: Elijah—1 Kings 17—19.
    Group Two: Elisha—2 Kings 1—6.

• After both groups have presented their dramas or mimes, discuss:

What godly qualities do you see in both prophets' lives? How would people today respond to such prophetic qualities in people?

• After this discussion, list the types of prophetic messages and ask people to share an example of one that they have seen in the prophets.

OPTION TWO: (FOR A 90-MINUTE SESSION)

The Character of the Prophets (15 Minutes)

• Ask everyone in the group to choose one prophet. Give them five minutes to skim their chosen book for the answers to the following questions.

What clues does this book give us about the prophet's character?

What is the main theme of this prophet's message?

How would this prophet be received today by the Church?

• After everyone has had time to survey the books, then invite them to share about their particular prophet.

SECTION THREE: GOD'S SON (10 MINUTES)

JESUS CHRIST REVEALED AS THE FULFILLMENT OF PROPHECY

• Divide the class into two groups. Give each group a large piece of newsprint or poster board and a felt-tip pen. The first group is to turn to Isaiah 53 and list every quality about Jesus' life that they find. The second group is to use the concordance and list every verse in the Gospel of Matthew in which Jesus refers to the words "prophet,"

GOD'S STORY IN THE PROPHETS

1. A prophet is God's mouthpiece. A prophet speaks God's Word to His people.

    Notes:

2. A popular notion about prophets is that they primarily foretell the future. Actually, a better way to describe prophets is that they walk with God so closely that God reveals to them what He is about to do. Prophets boldly "forthtell" God's Word about both the present and the future.

    Notes:

3. Certain major themes dominate most of the prophets.

    Notes:

4. The prophetic books point to the coming kingdom of God established by the Messiah. Messiah means "anointed one."

    Notes:

CONTINUED

Before the next session, read:

Sunday: God's Case Against Judah (Isaiah 1:1-18)

Monday: Isaiah's Commission (Isaiah 6:1-13)

Tuesday: Christ—Israel's Hope (Isaiah 7:10-16; 9:1-21)

Wednesday: The Coming Kingdom (Isaiah 11:1-16)

Thursday: A Great God (Isaiah 40:1-31)

Friday: Christ—Our Substitute (Isaiah 53:1-12)

Saturday: A Glorious Salvation (Isaiah 55:1-13)

TIMES OF THE PROPHETS

Books of Major Prophets

Isaiah	Jeremiah	Lamentations	Ezekiel	Daniel

The Books of Minor Prophets

Hosea	Joel	Amos	Obadiah	Jonah	Micah	Nahum	Habakkuk	Zephaniah	Haggai	Zechariah	Malachi

Israel's prophets are a built-in "reformation" aspect of Old Testament faith. The word "prophet" means "to speak out"—to *forth-tell* God's word as much as to foretell the future. They spoke out against hypocrisy, injustice, immorality and idolatry, warning God's people that He would punish them for such continued disobedience. The prophets also foretold the time when God would save a remnant of His people through whom all nations would be blessed.

© 1996 BY GOSPEL LIGHT. PERMISSION TO PHOTOCOPY GRANTED.

Understanding Isaiah

The purpose of this session is:

- To provide an overview of the book of Isaiah;
- To discover how Jesus Christ is revealed in Isaiah as the Messiah.

In this session, group members will learn:

- Key truths about God's story in Isaiah;
- That Jesus Christ is revealed in Isaiah;
- The basic principle of God's judgment and exile for continued sin and His promise of restoration through the Messiah;
- How to apply the truths revealed in Isaiah to their own lives.

KEY VERSES

"'Come now, let us reason together,' says the LORD. 'Though your sins are like scarlet, they shall be as white as snow; though they are red as crimson, they shall be like wool. If you are willing and obedient, you will eat the best from the land; but if you resist and rebel, you will be devoured by the sword.' For the mouth of the Lord has spoken." Isaiah 1:18-20

"For to us a child is born, to us a son is given, and the government will be on his shoulders, and he will be called Wonderful Counselor, Mighty God, Everlasting Father, Prince of Peace." Isaiah 9:6

"But he was pierced for our transgressions, he was crushed for our iniquities; the punishment that brought us peace was upon him, and by his wounds we are healed. We all, like sheep, have gone astray, each of us has turned to his own way; and the LORD has laid on him the iniquity of us all." Isaiah 53:5,6

BEFORE THE SESSION

- Pray for group members by name, asking the Holy Spirit to teach the spiritual truths in Isaiah to them.
- Read chapter 18 in *What the Bible Is All About*.
- Prepare copies of Session 6 handouts, "God's Story in Isaiah," and "Messianic Prophecies in Isaiah."
- Check off the following supplies once you have secured them:

_____ A chalkboard and chalk or a flip chart or overhead projector with markers.

_____ Extra Bibles, pencils and paper for group members.

- If you are having a 90-minute session, carefully read the two option sections right now and pull together any supplies you need for them.
- Read the entire session and look up every passage. Have your Bible *Tuck-In*™ page ready for yourself.
- Arrive early and be ready to warmly greet each group member as he or she arrives.
- Memorize the key verses. Share them periodically as you teach the session and ask the group to repeat them.

SECTION ONE: GOD'S STORY (20 MINUTES)

GOD'S STORY IN ISAIAH

Objective: To tell God's story in these books so that Christians will apply the truths from Isaiah to their own lives.

Greet everyone as they arrive. Tell the following story doing the suggested activities as you come to them. Distribute the handout "God's Story In Isaiah" to group members.

What distinguished the true prophets from the false prophets in the Old Testament?

True prophets were consistently accurate (see Deuteronomy 18:21,22). **Their prophesying and teaching led people to worship the true Lord alone** (see Deuteronomy 18:15-20; cf. 13:2,3) **and they bore good fruit in their lives and ministries** (see the contrasts in Jeremiah 23:10,11,14).

False prophets were presumptuous in attitude, they bore bad fruit in their lives and they were consistently inaccurate in their prophecies (see Jeremiah 23:10-22; Ezekiel 13:10-19). **When they managed to get a prophecy right, their teaching led people away from the one true God** (see Deuteronomy 13:1-5; 18:20-22).

Have everyone read Deuteronomy 18:18,19 as you read it out loud. Discuss the following with the group:

Are there prophets like Moses, Elijah, Isaiah and the others today?

Many people claim to be prophets today. What distinguishes God's prophets from false prophets?

If someone shared a "word from God" with you, how would you judge that person's prophecy? How should you act toward that person?

Old Testaments prophets were persecuted when they would forthtell the truth, no matter how painful that truth might be. How do you think the Church might treat prophets like Isaiah today?

God's Word came to prophets in dreams, visions and everyday experiences that God communicated to His people through the prophet.

Isaiah had a vision of the throne of God in chapter 6. He spoke "oracles" from God, or verbal pronouncements from God to His people and to the nations of the earth (see chapters 13—24). The ordinary experience of naming a child gave rise to prophecy when Isaiah's sons were given names as prophetic pronouncements to Israel (see vv. 7:3; 8:3).

Discuss the following with the whole group:

How does God reveal Himself today to His people?

How can we know that a particular revelation is truly from God?

Isaiah was born in the middle of the eighth century B.C. about the same time as the founding of the Roman Empire by Romulus and Remus and the founding of Sparta and Athens in Greece.

Isaiah had a significant impact on the royal court of his day as he was both a counselor to the king (see Isaiah 37:1-7) and a scribe (see 2 Chronicles 26:22). His words were unpopular and his actions unusual as he delivered God's Word.

Have the class imagine Isaiah delivering an address that sounds like Isaiah 1:1-20 to a joint session of the Congress of the United States. Read the passage to the whole group. Have them survey these twenty verses and then help you list all the sins that God specifically mentions in these verses on the board, flip chart or overhead. Circle those sins that the group members believe are particularly relevant to America today. Discuss how such a prophetic judgment would be received in our nation today. (Do not erase your list. You will use it later in the session.)

Read Isaiah 20 together. Ask: **How would society and the Church respond to Isaiah's actions?**

Isaiah has two distinct emphases which cause some scholars to believe that there was more than one author.

In the first part of the book (chapters 1—39), **God delivers judgment on His people and the nations of the earth through Isaiah. In the second part of the book** (chapters 40—66), **God reveals the coming Messiah and His kingdom.**

Divide the class into two groups. Have one group survey the first 39 chapters of Isaiah and jot down the major themes they find in these chapters. Have the second group survey chapters 40 through 66 and jot down those themes. Then with the whole group share what they have discovered. Point out that just as the Old Testament opens with God's case against man caused by sin, Isaiah parallels that theme. The second half of Isaiah parallels the New Testament revelation of the Messiah and God's grace. Isaiah like Revelation concludes with a vision of the new heaven and the new earth where the righteousness of God will reign.

Isaiah's message warned Judah about rebellion, greed, faulty political alliances and idolatry.

Through Isaiah, God told Judah her only security was in Him. God promised judgment and exile for sin. He also promised forgiveness and restoration for repentance (see Isaiah 26:19-21).

Discuss: **What forms of rebellion and idolatry do we practice as a nation?** Focus the discussion on the ways we are similar to ancient Judah.

While Isaiah warned Judah of God's impending judgment and exile, he also spoke of the coming restoration of Israel.

The future glory of God's people, an era of prosperity and the reign of the Messiah are promised in Isaiah 60—66. His prophecy of the suffering Servant in Isaiah 53 will be studied later in this session.

OPTION ONE: (FOR A 90-MINUTE SESSION)

God's Kingdom of Righteousness (15 Minutes)

Two magnificent visions of the coming kingdom of God are revealed in Isaiah 24—26 and Isaiah 61—66.

Divide the whole group into two groups. Ask everyone in the smaller groups to select one section of the passages from the following assignments.

Group One: Isaiah 24—26; 1 Corinthians 15:35-58; Revelation 20—22; Mark 13.

Group Two: Isaiah 61—66; Luke 4:14-21; Matthew 5:1-12, Revelation 20—22; Matthew 24.

Ask the groups to survey their assigned passages together and then answer the questions on their handouts.

SECTION TWO: GOD'S PERSON (10 MINUTES)

ISAIAH: "HERE AM I, SEND ME"

Isaiah lived under the reigns of four kings of Judah. He preached in Jerusalem and counseled in the courts of Uzziah, Jotham, Ahaz and Hezekiah.

Divide the whole group into groups of three. Have each person in each small group take one of these assignments:

Person One: Isaiah Under Uzziah and Jotham (Isaiah 1—6)
Person Two: Isaiah Under Ahaz (Isaiah 7—14)
Person Three: Isaiah Under Hezekiah (Isaiah 15—39)

Take five minutes to skim over what Isaiah did and said in each king's reign. Then ask each person to report back to his or her small group using the following questions to help summarize:

How did Isaiah speak God's Word to this king?

How was Isaiah treated during this king's reign?

How was Isaiah faithful to his calling under all the kings (see chapter 6)?

OPTION TWO: (FOR A 90-MINUTE SESSION)

Jesus' Suffering for Us (15 Minutes)

Have group members form pairs. Ask the pairs to read all of Isaiah 53. Tell them that while they are reading, they are to select three verses that fit the following guidelines. Write the guidelines on the board, flip chart or overhead.

One verse that touches you deeply.

One verse that you would share with someone about why Jesus died.

One verse that gives you great hope.

With the whole group, have them share their completion of the following sentence:

To me the suffering and crucifixion means that _____.

SECTION THREE: GOD'S SON (20 MINUTES)

JESUS CHRIST REVEALED AS THE MESSIAH

Objective: To discover how Jesus is portrayed as Messiah in Isaiah.

Ask everyone to turn to the section "Messianic Prophecies in Isaiah" on their handouts. Have everyone form groups of four. Divide the prophecies evenly among the groups. Give them 10 minutes to match all the prophecies. Then give them the following answers: 1=f, 2=j, 3=l, 4=i, 5=m, 6=h, 7=g, 8=a, 9=b, 10=e, 11=d, 12=o, 13=s, 14=t, 15=gg, 16=hh, 17=bb, 18=cc, 19=ee, 20=n, 21=p, 22=u, 23=dd, 24=z, 25=w, 26=ii, 27=jj, 28=kk, 29=ff, 30=v, 31=r and 32=q.

With the whole group discuss:

Which prophecies did you discover in Isaiah that you never knew about?
What feelings do you have as you see just how much Jesus fulfilled prophecy?
How would you use prophecies like these in witnessing to a Gentile? To a Jew?

PURSUING GOD (5 MINUTES)

NEXT STEPS I NEED TO TAKE

Objective: To take a realistic assessment of one's relationship with Jesus and how that relationship might grow closer in the coming week.

Ask everyone to look at the list of sins that was listed on the board earlier (during Section One) from Isaiah 1.

Have everyone find a partner. Invite the partners to choose one sin that they personally feel convicted about and one sin that needs to be confessed on behalf of the nation. Pray together about those sins.

PRAYER (5 MINUTES)

Objective: To seek to hear God's voice and pray as Isaiah did in Isaiah 6.

Isaiah's conversion experience in chapter 6 reveals a powerful prayer relationship with God. The stages of this prayer were: (Write the following list on the board.)

Confession: (6:5)
Cleansing: (6:7)
Consecration: (6:8)
Commission: (6:9)

In the same pairs, ask each person to pray through these stages using the following sentences:

Lord, I confess _____.

Lord, cleanse me from _____.

Lord, consecrate me to _____.

Lord, I am available and ready to go _____.

After the pairs are finished praying, close with the whole group in a corporate prayer based on Isaiah 6. A model for this prayer might be:

> **Lord Jesus, we confess our sin and receive Your cleansing through Your shed blood. Consecrate us by Your Spirit to go where You send us as Your witnesses and servants, in Jesus' name. Amen.**

Session 6 Bible *Tuck-In*™

UNDERSTANDING ISAIAH

The purpose of this session is:

- To provide an overview of the book of Isaiah;
- To discover how Jesus Christ is revealed as the Messiah.

KEY VERSES

"'Come now, let us reason together,' says the LORD. 'Though your sins are like scarlet, they shall be as white as snow; though they are red as crimson, they shall be like wool. If you are willing and obedient, you will eat the best from the land; but if you resist and rebel, you will be devoured by the sword.' For the mouth of the Lord has spoken." Isaiah 1:18-20

"For to us a child is born, to us a son is given, and the government will be on his shoulders, and he will be called Wonderful Counselor, Mighty God, Everlasting Father, Prince of Peace." Isaiah 9:6

"But he was pierced for our transgressions, he was crushed for our iniquities; the punishment that brought us peace was upon him, and by his wounds we are healed. We all, like sheep, have gone astray, each of us has turned to his own way; and the LORD has laid on him the iniquity of us all." Isaiah 53:5,6

------ Fold ------

95

---

knew were in Isaiah? What feelings do you have as you see just how much Jesus fulfilled prophecy? How would you use prophecies like these in witnessing to a Gentile? to a Jew?

PURSUING GOD (5 MINUTES)

NEXT STEPS I NEED TO TAKE

- Ask everyone to look at the list of sins from Isaiah 1 that you listed on the board earlier.
- In pairs, invite them to choose one sin that they personally feel convicted about and one sin that needs to be confessed on behalf of the nation. Have them pray together about those sins.

PRAYER (5 MINUTES)

- Isaiah's conversion experience in chapter 6 reveals a powerful prayer relationship with God. The stages of this prayer are: (Write these on the board.)

  Confession: (6:5)   Consecration: (6:8)
  Cleansing: (6:7)   Commission: (6:9)

- In pairs, ask each person to pray through these stages using the following sentences:

  Lord, I confess _____ •

  Lord, cleanse me from _____ •

  Lord, consecrate me to _____ •

  Lord, I am available and ready to go _____ •

- After the pairs are finished praying, close with the whole group in a corporate prayer based on Isaiah 6. A model for this prayer might be:

Lord Jesus, we confess our sin and receive Your cleansing through Your shed blood. Consecrate us by Your Spirit to go where You send us as Your witnesses and servants, in Jesus' name. Amen.

SECTION ONE: GOD'S STORY (20 MINUTES)

GOD'S STORY IN ISAIAH

- Greet everyone as they arrive. Tell the group the Bible story in Isaiah, doing the suggested activities as you come to them. Distribute the handout "God's Story In Isaiah" to group members.

OPTION ONE: (FOR A 90-MINUTE SESSION)

God's Kingdom of Righteousness (15 Minutes)

- Divide the whole group into two groups. Ask everyone in the smaller groups to select one section of the passages from the following assignments.

Group One: Isaiah 24—26; 1 Corinthians 15:35-58; Revelation 20—22; Mark 13.

Group Two: Isaiah 61—66; Luke 4:14-21; Matthew 5:1-12, Revelation 20—22; Matthew 24.

- Ask the groups to survey their passages together and then to answer the questions on their handouts.

SECTION TWO: GOD'S PERSON (10 MINUTES)

ISAIAH: "HERE AM I, SEND ME"

- Divide the whole group into groups of three. Have each person in the small groups take one of these assignments:

Person One: Isaiah Under Uzziah and Jotham (Isaiah 1—6)
Person Two: Isaiah Under Ahaz (Isaiah 7—14)
Person Three: Isaiah Under Hezekiah (Isaiah 15—39)

- Take five minutes to skim over what Isaiah did and said in each king's reign. Then ask each person to report back to

his or her small group using the following questions to help summarize:

How did Isaiah speak God's Word to this King?
How was Isaiah treated during this king's reign?
How was Isaiah faithful to his calling under all the kings (see chapter 6)?

OPTION TWO: (FOR A 90-MINUTE SESSION)

Jesus' Suffering for Us (15 Minutes)

- Form pairs. Ask the pairs to read Isaiah 53. While they are reading, they are to select three verses that fit the following guidelines. Write the guidelines on the board, flip chart or overhead.

One verse that touches you deeply.
One verse that you would share with someone about why Jesus died.
One verse that gives you great hope.

- Have the group share their completions of the following:
To me the suffering and crucifixion means that _____.

SECTION THREE: GOD'S SON (20 MINUTES)

JESUS CHRIST REVEALED AS THE MESSIAH

- Refer to the section on their handouts titled "Messianic Prophecies in Isaiah." Divide into groups of four. Divide the prophecies evenly among the groups. Give them 10 minutes to match all the prophecies. Answers: 1=f, 2=j, 3=l, 4=i, 5=m, 6=h, 7=g, 8=a, 9=b, 10=e, 11=o, 12=o, 13=s, 14=t, 15=gg, 16=hh, 17=bb, 18=cc, 19=ee, 20=n, 21=p, 22=u, 23=dd, 24=z, 25=w, 26=ii, 27=jj, 28=kk, 29=ff, 30=v, 31=r and 32=q.)

- Discuss: Which prophecies did you discover that you never

GOD'S STORY IN ISAIAH

1. What distinguished the true prophets from the false prophets in the Old Testament?

   Notes:

2. God's Word came to prophets in dreams, visions and everyday experiences that God communicated to His people through the prophet.

   Notes:

3. Isaiah had a significant impact on the royal court of his day as he was both a counselor to the king (see Isaiah 37:1-7) and a scribe (see 2 Chronicles 26:22). His words were unpopular and his actions unusual as he delivered God's Word.

   Notes:

4. Isaiah has two distinct emphases which cause some scholars to believe that there was more than one author.

   Notes:

5. Isaiah's message warned Judah about rebellion, greed, faulty political alliances and idolatry.

   Notes:

CONTINUED

6. While Isaiah warned Judah of God's impending judgment and exile, he also spoke of the coming restoration of Israel.

Notes:

GOD'S KINGDOM OF RIGHTEOUSNESS

What are five central characteristics of God's kingdom in Isaiah?

1. _____
2. _____
3. _____
4. _____
5. _____

What are five central characteristics of God's kingdom in the New Testament?

1. _____
2. _____
3. _____
4. _____
5. _____

Before the next session, read:
Sunday: Jeremiah Warns Judah (Jeremiah 1:1-10; 2:1-13; 3:12,22,23; 4:14-19; 6:1-30)
Monday: A Rebuke (Jeremiah 7:1-15; 9:1-16; 17:5-18)
Tuesday: The Potter (Jeremiah 18:1-17)
Wednesday: The Faithless Shepherds (Jeremiah 23:1-40)
Thursday: Repentance and Restoration (Jeremiah 24—25)
Friday: Israel's Last Days (Jeremiah 30:18-31:40)
Saturday: The Overthrow of Judah (Jeremiah 52:1-34); Comfort to the Sorrowing
(Lamentations 1—5)

MESSIANIC PROPHECIES IN ISAIAH

Match the subject of these prophecies with the correct passage.

___ 1. At the Messiah's coming, nations would repent.

___ 2. Hearts would be hardened at His coming.

___ 3. Messiah would be born of a virgin.
___ 4. He would be offensive to the religious.
___ 5. Messiah would be called Immanuel.
___ 6. He would come as a child, a son given to us.
___ 7. A government would be on His shoulders.

___ 8. God's Spirit would anoint Him to preach liberty.
___ 9. He would be full of wisdom and power.

___ 10. He would come from David's household.

___ 11. In Him, death would be swallowed in victory.

___ 12. The deaf would hear, the blind see.

___ 13. One would come before, making the way ready.

___ 14. As a shepherd, He would tend His sheep.

___ 15. He would be pierced for our transgressions.

___ 16. He would suffer for us.

___ 17. He would be scourged and spat upon.

___ 18. He would be rejected and insulted.
___ 19. He would be crucified with transgressors.

___ 20. He would be the stone in Zion.

___ 21. He would heal the needy.

a. Isa. 11:2; 42:1; Matt. 3:16; John 1:32

b. Isa. 11:1-10; Rom. 15:12; Eph. 1:17

c. Isa. 16:4-5; Luke 1:31-33

d. Isa. 25:6-12; 1 Cor. 15:54

e. Isa. 22:21-25; Rev. 3:7

f. Isa. 2:2-4; Luke 24:47.

g. Isa. 9:6; Matt. 28:18; 1 Cor. 15:24-25

h. Isa. 9:6; John 3:16

i. Isa. 8:14, 15; Rom. 9:33; 1 Pet. 2:8

j. Isa. 6:9-10; Matt. 13:14-15; John 12:39,40

k. Isa. 9:1-2; Matt. 4:14; Luke 2:32

l. Isa. 7:14; Mt. 1:22-23; Luke 1:27-35

m. Isa. 7:14; 8:8,10; Matt. 1:21,23; John 14:8-10

n. Isa. 28:16; Rom. 9:33; 1 Pet. 2:6

o. Isa. 29:18,19; Matt. 11:5; Mark 7:37

p. Isa. 35:4-10; Matt. 9:30; John 9:1-7

q. Isa. 65:17-25; 2 Pet. 3:13; Rev. 21:1

r. Isa. 63:8-9; Matt. 25:34-40

s. Isa. 40:3-5; Matt. 3:3; John 1:23

t. Isa. 40:10,11; John 10:11; Heb. 13:20

u. Isa. 42:1-4; Matt. 12:17-21; Phil. 2:7

CONTINUED

___ 22. Messiah would be a meek servant.

___ 23. He would call the Gentiles.

___ 24. The nations would walk in His light.

___ 25. He would come as a king.

___ 26. He would be a lamb slaughtered for us.

___ 27. Messiah would be silent when accused.

___ 28. He would be buried with the rich.

___ 29. He would bear our iniquities and forgive sins.

___ 30. His clothing would be bloodied.

___ 31. He would be afflicted with the afflicted.

___ 32. He would usher in a new heaven and earth.

v. Isa. 63:1-3; Rev. 19:13

w. Isa. 62:11; Matt. 21:5; Rev. 22:12

x. Isa. 49:6; Luke 2:32; Acts 13:47

y. Isa. 61:1-3; Luke 4:17-19; Acts 10:38

z. Isa. 61:1-3; Luke 2:32

aa. Isa. 59:16-20; Rom. 11:26-27

bb. Isa. 50:6; Matt. 26:67; John 19:1

cc. Isa. 53:3; Matt. 27:1,2; Luke 18:31-33

dd. Isa. 55:4,5; Rom 9:25; Rev. 1:5

ee. Isa. 53:12; Mark 15:27,28

ff. Isa. 53:11; Acts 10:43; 1 Cor. 15:3

gg. Isa. 53:5; Rom. 4:25; 2 Cor. 5:21

hh. Isa. 53:4,5; Matt. 8:17; Luke 23:32-35

ii. Isa. 53:7, John 1:29

jj. Isa. 53:7; Matt. 26:62

kk. Isa. 53:9; Matt. 27:57-60

Understanding Jeremiah and Lamentations

The purpose of this session is:

- To provide an overview of the books of Jeremiah and Lamentations;
- To discover how Jesus Christ is revealed in Jeremiah and Lamentations as the Righteous Branch.

In this session, group members will learn:

- Key truths about God's story in these books;
- That Jesus Christ is revealed in Jeremiah and Lamentations;
- The basic principle that God can use anyone no matter their age, position or abilities to deliver His message of judgment for sinners and restoration for the repentant;
- How to apply the truths revealed in Jeremiah and Lamentations to their own lives.

KEY VERSES

"Woe is me, my mother, that thou hast borne me a man of strife and a man of contention to the whole earth!" Jeremiah 15:10, *KJV*

"'The days are coming,' declares the LORD, 'when I will raise up to David a righteous Branch, a King who will reign wisely and do what is just and right in the land." Jeremiah 23:5

"Because of the LORD's great love we are not consumed, for his compassions never fail. They are new every morning; great is your faithfulness, I say to myself, 'The LORD is my portion; therefore I will wait for him.'" Lamentations 3:22-24

BEFORE THE SESSION

- Pray for group members by name, asking the Holy Spirit to teach the spiritual truths in Jeremiah and Lamentations to them.
- Read chapter 19 in *What the Bible Is All About*.
- Prepare copies of Session 7 handout "God's Story in Jeremiah and Lamentations."

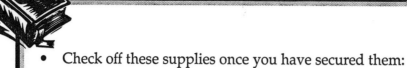

- Check off these supplies once you have secured them:
  - ____ A chalkboard and chalk or a flip chart or an overhead projector with markers;
  - ____ Extra Bibles, pencils and paper for group members.
  - ____ Put up six pieces of newsprint or poster board on the walls around the room. Number them from one to six.
- If you are having a 90-minute session, carefully read the two option sections right now and pull together any supplies you need for them.
- Read the entire session and look up every passage. Have your Bible *Tuck-In*™ page ready for yourself.
- Arrive early and be ready to warmly greet each group member as he or she arrives.
- Memorize the key verses. Share them periodically and ask the group to repeat them as you teach the session.

SECTION ONE: GOD'S STORY (20 MINUTES)

GOD'S STORY IN JEREMIAH AND LAMENTATIONS

Objective: To tell God's story in these books so that Christians will apply the truths from Jeremiah and Lamentations to their own lives.

Greet everyone as they arrive. Tell the following story doing the suggested activities as you come to them. Distribute the handout "God's Story in Jeremiah and Lamentations" to group members.

Display an overhead transparency of the "Times of the Prophets" handout from Session 5 so that the group may see where Jeremiah is on the time line.

The young man, Jeremiah, son of the priest Hilkiah, became God's instrument to give His Word of rebuke and judgment to Judah.

He lived at the end of the sixth century B.C. and into the fifth century B.C. Unlike many of the prophets, he has told us much about himself (see Jeremiah 1).

Ask everyone in the group to turn to Jeremiah 1 and read through the information about him. With the whole group, list on the board the things this chapter reveals about Jeremiah.

The book of Jeremiah is not chronological.

He prophesied about...

Judah: Captivity and restoration;

Particular cities: Jerusalem, Babylon and Damascus;

Gentile nations: Egypt, Philistia, Moab, Ammon, Edom, Elam and Babylon;

The Messiah.

Jeremiah uses many common everyday objects and experiences as symbols or illustrations in his prophecies. God gave these objects or experiences His interpretation so that Jeremiah could warn and exhort God's people.

Assign the following passages to various group members. Ask them to look up the passage, discover what the object or experience is that God used, and briefly state the interpretation of that for Israel.

Jeremiah 1:11,12 (almond branch)

1:13-15 (boiling pot)

13:1-11 (ruined belt)

13:12,13 (full wineskin)

14:1-12 (drought)

18:1-6 (potter's clay)

19:1,10,11 (the broken jar)

24:1-10 (two baskets of figs)

27:1-12 (straps and crossbars)

32:6-15 (buying a field)

43:9-13 (hidden stones)

51:59-64 (sunken scroll)

Jeremiah delivered God's messages to five kings of Judah: Josiah, Jehoahaz, Jehoiakim, Jehoiachin and Zedekiah.

There were three great events in Jeremiah's life: the Battle of Megiddo in which King Josiah was killed; the Battle of Carchemish in which Egypt was defeated by Babylon and the first deportation of the Jews happened; and the capture of Jerusalem by Nebuchadnezzar in which the temple and the city were destroyed (2 Chronicles 35—36; Jeremiah 1; 16; 52).

Divide the whole group into two groups. Have one group turn to 2 Chronicles 35—36. Ask the second group to survey Jeremiah 1; 26; 52. Ask them to explore how Jeremiah communicated God's Word and how the king and people responded to Jeremiah. Have each group share what they have discovered and then discuss:

How did Israel treat her prophets?

How would Jeremiah be treated today in our culture?

During Jehoiakim's 11-year reign, much evil was done and Jeremiah suffered.

Jehoiakim heavily taxed Judah in order to pay tribute to Egypt. He was selfish and spent lavishly on himself and the palace (see Jeremiah 16:1-7).

Ask volunteers to read Jeremiah 23:9-40; 26:1-7; 2 Kings 23:35 aloud and then discuss:

What were some of Israel's sins during this period?

How did God declare He would deal with their sin?

One of the strongest prophecies of Jeremiah was delivered in the Temple.

His hearers were shocked and Jeremiah was viewed as unpatriotic. During the fourth year of Jehoiakim's reign, Jeremiah had the scribe, Baruch, write down his words even while he was imprisoned. Jeremiah then instructed Baruch to read the scroll in the Temple (see Jeremiah 36:1-10).

Have the whole group skim Jeremiah 36—38. Then discuss the following:

Why was Jeremiah persecuted so viciously?

What was his response to his persecutors and to God?

During the reign of Zedekiah, the last king of Judah, Jeremiah delivered God's word about the impending exile and the final restoration of Israel.

These prophecies all came true and to his sorrow, Jeremiah lived through the destruction of the Temple and Jerusalem as well as the exile of the Jews to Babylon in 586 B.C.

Divide the whole group into six smaller groups. Ask each group to read their assigned passages and then summarize the prophecies in their section in two sentences and write the summaries on the newsprint or poster board that you put up earlier on the wall.

> **Group One: Jeremiah 23; 31** (God's future dealings with Judah)
>
> **Group Two: Jeremiah 20:4** (Conquest by Nebuchadnezzar, king of Babylon)
>
> **Group Three: Jeremiah 25—26** (Judah's exile into Babylon for 70 years and return)
>
> **Group Four: Jeremiah 23:6; 30:4-11; 33:14-26** (Prophecy about the Messiah)
>
> **Group Five: Jeremiah 24** (The northern kingdom of Israel will be scattered among the nations)
>
> **Group Six: Jeremiah 23:1-40; 32:37-41** (Final recovery of Israel)

The book of Lamentations is composed of five beautiful poems in which Jeremiah mourns for God's people and sees God's grace ultimately shine through to save His people.

With the same six groups, have Group One split up and evenly distribute their members among the other five groups, then assign each group one of the five chapters of Lamentations. Ask the groups to find one passage in their assigned chapters that gives an example of Jeremiah's grief and one passage that offers hope in that chapter, then have all the groups share their verses.

OPTION ONE: (FOR A 90-MINUTE SESSION)

Lamentations (15 Minutes)

The book of Lamentations touches upon every sorrow and grief we might experience in our lives. With the whole group, skim the book and list on the board, flip chart or overhead all of the things that cause Jeremiah great sorrow. Then ask for two or three people to share a time when they have experienced sorrow or grief over a great loss in life and how God saw them through it and comforted them.

Have the group read 2 Corinthians 1:1-7 and then discuss:
How does God help us transform our pain into pearls?
Which verses in Lamentations are the most comforting?
What can we do to comfort others in their sorrow with God's comfort?

SECTION TWO: GOD'S PERSON (10 MINUTES)

JEREMIAH: BOLD PROPHET TO THE KINGS OF JUDAH
As with Elijah and other prophets, we see a genuine boldness in Jeremiah's life to speak God's Word no matter what the personal cost.

Go back to the five groups you had at the end of Section One. Make the following assignments:

Group One:	Jeremiah 1—10
Group Two:	Jeremiah 11—20
Group Three:	Jeremiah 21—30
Group Four:	Jeremiah 31—40
Group Five:	Jeremiah 41—52

Ask each group to look for two things: **A bold prophecy; and a time of sorrow or persecution in Jeremiah's life.** After the groups have had three to four minutes to survey their material, ask each group to share what they have discovered. Then with the whole group discuss:

Which groups were most often condemned by God through Jeremiah?

How did Jeremiah withstand the attacks against him?

OPTION TWO: (FOR A 90-MINUTE SESSION)

Jeremiah's Call and Commission (15 Minutes)

Ask the group members to read Jeremiah 1 and to identify the verses that describe Jeremiah's call to be a prophet and the verses which describe his reluctance to accept that call. The answers are:

> The Call: Jeremiah 1:2,4,5,7-19.
> Reluctance: Jeremiah 1:6

Write the following incomplete sentences on the board, flip chart or overhead while the group forms pairs. Ask each person to complete the following sentences with his or her partner:

One way I see God calling me is _____.

One reluctance I have in accepting His call is _____.

One way that God relieved Jeremiah's fear was _____.

The way I need God to help me deal with my fears is _____.

SECTION THREE: GOD'S SON (15 MINUTES)

JESUS CHRIST REVEALED AS THE RIGHTEOUS BRANCH

Objective: To discover how Jesus is portrayed as Messiah, the Righteous Branch in Jeremiah.

Have everyone find a partner. On their handouts are drawings of various prophecies about Jesus. Have the pairs first guess what that symbol represents in the Messiah's life. Then look up the texts and label each symbol with the text that speaks prophetically about the Messiah.

The following is a correct list for you to give the pairs when they are finished:

Spring of Living Waters — Jeremiah 2:13

Great Physician—Jeremiah 8:22

Good Shepherd—Jeremiah 31:10;

Righteous Branch—Jeremiah 23:5

Davidic King Who Is Raised Up—Jeremiah 30:9

The Redeemer—Jeremiah 50:34

The Lord, Our Righteousness—Jeremiah 23:6

PURSUING GOD (5 MINUTES)

NEXT STEPS I NEED TO TAKE

Objective: To take a realistic assessment of one's relationship with Jesus and how that relationship might grow closer in the coming week.

One of the most familiar passages from Jeremiah is the experience he had watching a potter who shaped, broke and reshaped a pot.

Have everyone remain in pairs. Ask each pair to read Jeremiah 18:1-6 together. Say: **Turn to the handout section entitled "At the Potter's House" and put your own name on the pot that most represents your experience with the Lord right now. After you put your name on one of the pots, share with your partner how you labeled your handout and why.**

PRAYER (5 MINUTES)

Objective: To pray through Lamentations 3:23-26.

Invite each person to write a personal prayer based on Lamentations 3:22-26 in the space provided on the handout.

Ask two or three volunteers to share their prayers as closing prayers for the group.

Session 7 Bible *Tuck-In*™

UNDERSTANDING JEREMIAH AND LAMENTATIONS

The purpose of this session is:

- To provide an overview of the books of Jeremiah and Lamentations;
- To discover how Jesus Christ is revealed as the Righteous Branch.

KEY VERSES

"Woe is me, my mother, that thou hast borne me a man of strife and a man of contention to the whole earth!" Jeremiah 15:10, *KJV*

"'The days are coming,' declares the LORD, 'when I will raise up to David a righteous Branch, a King who will reign wisely and do what is just and right in the land.'" Jeremiah 23:5

"Because of the LORD's great love we are not consumed, for his compassions never fail. They are new every morning; great is your faithfulness. I say to myself, 'The LORD is my portion; therefore I will wait for him.'" Lamentations 3:22-24

SECTION THREE: GOD'S SON (15 MINUTES)

JESUS CHRIST REVEALED AS THE RIGHTEOUS BRANCH

- Have everyone find a partner. On their handouts are drawings of various prophecies about Jesus. Have the pairs first guess what that symbol represents in the Messiah's life, then look up the texts and label each symbol with the text that speaks prophetically about the Messiah.
- When they have finished, share the correct answers with them.

PURSUING GOD (5 MINUTES)

NEXT STEPS I NEED TO TAKE

- Have them remain in pairs. Ask each pair to read Jeremiah 18:1-6 together. Say: **Look at your handout sheets and put your own name on the pot that most represents your experience with the Lord right now. After you put your name on one of the pots, share with your partner how you labeled your handout and why.**

PRAYER (5 MINUTES)

- Invite each person to write a personal prayer based on Lamentations 3:22-26 in the space provided on the handout.
- Ask two or three volunteers to share their prayers as closing prayers for the group.

SECTION ONE: GOD'S STORY (20 MINUTES)

GOD'S STORY IN JEREMIAH AND LAMENTATIONS

- Greet everyone as they arrive. Tell the Bible story in Jeremiah and Lamentations, doing the suggested activities as you come to them. Distribute the handout "God's Story In Jeremiah and Lamentations" to group members.

- Display an overhead transparency of the "Times of the Prophets" handout from Session 5 so that the group may see where Jeremiah is on the time line.

OPTION ONE: (FOR A 90-MINUTE SESSION)

Lamentations (15 Minutes)

- With the whole group, skim the book and list on the board all of the things that caused Jeremiah great sorrow. Then ask for two or three people to share a time when they have experienced sorrow or grief over a great loss in life and how God saw them through it and comforted them.

- As a group read 2 Corinthians 1:1-7, then discuss:
  How does God help us transform our pain into pearls?
  Which verses in Lamentations are the most comforting?
  What can we do to comfort others in their sorrow with God's comfort?

SECTION TWO: GOD'S PERSON (10 MINUTES)

JEREMIAH: BOLD PROPHET TO THE KINGS OF JUDAH

- Go back to the five groups you had at the end of Section One. Make these assignments:

Group One:	Jeremiah 1—10
Group Two:	Jeremiah 11—20
Group Three:	Jeremiah 21—30
Group Four:	Jeremiah 31—40
Group Five:	Jeremiah 41—52

- Ask each group to look for two things: **A bold prophecy and a time of sorrow or persecution in Jeremiah's life.**

- After the groups have had three to four minutes to survey their material, ask each group to share what they have discovered. Then with the whole group discuss:
  Which groups were most often condemned by God through Jeremiah?
  How did Jeremiah withstand the attacks against him?

OPTION TWO: FOR A 90-MINUTE SESSION

Jeremiah's Call and Commission (15 Minutes)

- Ask group members to read Jeremiah 1 and to identify the verses that describe Jeremiah's call to be a prophet and the verses which describe his reluctance to accept that call. The answers are:

  The Call: Jeremiah 1:2,4-6,7-19.
  Reluctance: Jeremiah 1:6

- Write the following incomplete sentences on the board, flip chart or overhead while the group forms pairs. Ask each person to complete the following sentences with his or her partner:

  One way I see God calling me is _____.
  One reluctance I have in accepting His call is _____.
  One way that God relieved Jeremiah's fear was _____.
  The way I need God to help me deal with my fears is _____.

GOD'S STORY IN JEREMIAH AND LAMENTATIONS

1. The young man, Jeremiah, son of priest Hilkiah, became God's instrument to give His Word of rebuke and judgment to Judah.

   Notes:

2. The book of Jeremiah is not chronological. He prophesied about...
   Judah: Captivity and restoration;
   Particular cities: Jerusalem, Babylon and Damascus;
   Gentile nations: Egypt, Philistia, Moab, Ammon, Edom, Elam and Babylon;
   The Messiah.

   Notes:

3. Jeremiah delivered God's messages to five kings of Judah: Josiah, Jehoahaz, Jehoiakim, Jehoiachin and Zedekiah.

   Notes:

4. During Jehoiakim's 11-year reign much evil was done and Jeremiah suffered.

   Notes:

CONTINUED

5. One of the strongest prophecies of Jeremiah was delivered in the Temple.

   Notes:

6. During the reign of Zedekiah, the last king of Judah, Jeremiah delivered God's word about the impending exile and the final restoration of Israel.

   Notes:

7. The book of Lamentations is composed of five beautiful poems in which Jeremiah mourns for God's people and sees God's grace ultimately shine through to save His people.

   Notes:

JESUS IN JEREMIAH

The seven symbols illustrated here represent seven attributes related to the coming Messiah found in Jeremiah. Try to guess what the symbols stand for in relationship to the Messiah. Then look up each passage and match it with the symbol. Finally, share with your partner which symbol is most meaningful to you and why.

| Jeremiah 2:13 | Jeremiah 8:22 | Jeremiah 23:5 | Jeremiah 23:6 |
| Jeremiah 30:9 | Jeremiah 31:10 | Jeremiah 50:34 | |

CONTINUED

AT THE POTTER'S HOUSE

In Jeremiah 18:1-6, we see a powerful image that God gave to Israel which we can apply to our own lives. The following pots are in various stages of formation that describe how your relationship with God is doing and how He is working in your life right now. Write your name on the pot that best describes you at this time in your life. Then share with your partner how you labeled your pot and why you see yourself there right now.

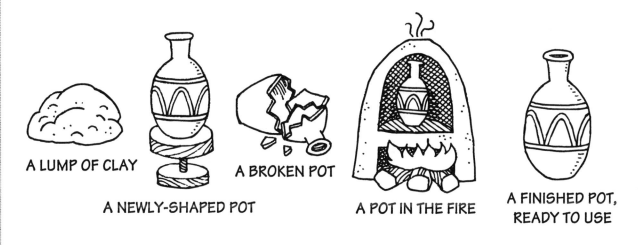

A LUMP OF CLAY

A NEWLY-SHAPED POT

A BROKEN POT

A POT IN THE FIRE

A FINISHED POT, READY TO USE

Write a prayer in response to Lamentations 3:22-26:

Before the next session read:
Sunday: The Prophet's Call (Ezekiel 2:1—3:9)
Monday: The Prophet—A Watchman (Ezekiel 3:10-27)
Tuesday: Israel Shall Be Saved (Ezekiel 11:14-21; 28:25,26)
Wednesday: Israel's Sins (Ezekiel 22:3-31;
Thursday: Israel's Future (Ezekiel 34:1-31)
Friday: Israel's Restoration (Ezekiel 36:1-38)
Saturday: Vision of the Dry Bones (Ezekiel 37:1-14)

Understanding Ezekiel

The purpose of this session is:

- To provide an overview of the book of Ezekiel;
- To discover how Jesus Christ is revealed in Ezekiel as the Son of Man.

In this session, group members will learn:

- Key truths about God's story in Ezekiel;
- That Jesus Christ is revealed in Ezekiel;
- The basic principle that God is acting in history to fulfill all of His promises to His people;
- How to apply the truths revealed in Ezekiel to their own lives.

KEY VERSES

"Son of man, I [God] have made you a watchman for the house of Israel; so hear the word I speak and give them warning from me." Ezekiel 33:7

"I will give you a new heart and put a new spirit in you; I will remove from you your heart of stone and give you a heart of flesh. And I will put my Spirit in you and move you to follow my decrees and be careful to keep my laws." Ezekiel 36:26,27

"Therefore prophesy and say to [Israel]: 'This is what the Sovereign LORD says: O my people, I am going to open your graves and bring you back up from them; I will bring you back to the land of Israel. Then you, my people, will know that I am the LORD, when I open your graves and bring you up from them.'" Ezekiel 37:12,13

BEFORE THE SESSION

- Pray for group members by name, asking the Holy Spirit to teach the spiritual truths in Ezekiel to them.
- Read chapter 20 in *What the Bible Is All About*.
- Prepare copies of Session 8 handout "God's Story in Ezekiel."
- Check off these supplies once you have secured them:
  - _____ A chalkboard and chalk or a flip chart or an overhead projector with markers;
  - _____ Extra Bibles, pencils and paper for group members;

_____ Five pieces of poster board and enough felt-tip pens for five groups to have five to seven colors each.

- If you are having a 90-minute session, carefully read the two option sections right now and pull together any supplies you need for them.
- Read the entire session and look up every passage. Have your Bible *Tuck-In*™ page ready for yourself.
- Arrive early and be ready to warmly greet each group member as he or she arrives.
- Memorize the key verses. Share them periodically and ask the group to repeat them as you teach the session.

SECTION ONE: GOD'S STORY (15 MINUTES)

GOD'S STORY IN EZEKIEL

Objective: To tell God's story so that Christians will apply the truths from Ezekiel to their own lives.

Greet everyone as they arrive. Tell the following story, doing the suggested activities as you come to them. Distribute the handout "God's Story In Ezekiel" to group members.

Display an overhead transparency of the "Times of the Prophets" handout from Session 5 so that the group may see where Ezekiel is on the time line.

While Jeremiah's ministry was concluding in Judah, the young prophet Ezekiel was already at work among the exiles in Babylon.

God needed a voice to warn the Jews and remind them of the reason that all of these calamities had befallen them. For 22 years, Ezekiel dealt with God's discouraged people in exile.

Have everyone read Ezekiel 1:1; 2:1-3; 3:1-9. Discuss the following questions:
How was Ezekiel's call similar to Jeremiah's? How was it different?
Reread Ezekiel 3:1-9. What does "eating the scroll" tell you about Ezekiel's call and authority as a prophet?

Ezekiel can minister to the Jews today by telling them that God will fulfill His trustworthy promises of restoring their land, their people and their Temple.

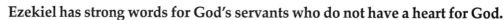

Ezekiel has strong words for God's servants who do not have a heart for God. Have various group members take turns reading Ezekiel 34 to the whole group. On the board, flip chart or overhead make two lists. Label one list: "Pastors/Shepherds should...." Label the other list: "Pastors/Shepherds should not...." Ask group members to call out the different attributes pastors should and should not possess based on Ezekiel 34, then discuss the following:

In what ways can we encourage our pastor(s)?

How can pastors be held accountable without being controlled or manipulated by others?

To the Christian, Ezekiel reveals God's purposes for Israel which demonstrate that He is acting in history to fulfill all of His promises.

Like Daniel and Revelation, Ezekiel is a visionary prophecy unfolding the end-time images and the promises of a new heaven and a new earth (see Ezekiel 37).

Ask the whole group to read through Ezekiel 37. Discuss the following:

What are some of the ways this prophecy has been fulfilled since the founding of Israel as a nation in 1948?

In what ways might the modern state of Israel be a sign of what God is doing in history?

Ezekiel and Daniel were young men ministering to the exiles in Babylon. God had told of Judah's captivity in Babylon more than 100 years before it happened (see Isaiah 39:6,7; Micah 4:10). Jeremiah had foretold a seventy-year captivity (see Jeremiah 25:11,12).

Ezekiel lived by the Chebar River, one of many canals built by the Babylonians that branches off the Euphrates River. To the pitiful Jews without a homeland and a temple, Ezekiel preached a message of comfort and hope using end-time, apocalyptic language which is language filled with symbols, visions, parables, poems, proverbs and prophecies of the end times.

Central to Ezekiel's prophecies was the glory of God. Ezekiel opens with heavenly glory in a vision and ends with the earthly glory of God's establishment of a new Israel and a new Temple (see Ezekiel 43:1-12).

Ask the group members to share their definitions of glory. Then have the group read Ezekiel 43:1-12. Have the group develop a description of what God's glory is according to Ezekiel. Ask group members to share experiences of God's glory that they may have had in their own lives.

God used Ezekiel to explain why He allowed His children to be exiled. Judah had been wicked and stiff-necked, guilty of unspeakable sin and abomination.

God used the nations of the world like Assyria, Babylon and Persia to be rods of judgment and correction. God was punishing His children for their sin and teaching them how to rely solely on Him (see Ezekiel 5:8-17).

Discuss:

How has God used other nations in our country's history to correct her ways?

How is our country like ancient Judah?

What does our nation rely upon other than God for our security?

Ezekiel prophesied the destruction of Jerusalem, the judgment against Israel's enemies, Judah's restoration and the golden age to come under the Messiah.

Ezekiel may be divided into three sections regarding the city of Jerusalem:

1. Pre-Siege (1—24): Ezekiel's prophecies for six years prior to the destruction of Jerusalem.
2. Siege (25—32): Prophecies about Israel's enemies and how God would deal with them.
3. Post-Siege (33—48): The restoration and reestablishment of Israel.

OPTION ONE: (FOR A 90-MINUTE SESSION)

THE GLORY OF GOD (15 MINUTES)

God's glory refers to His radiance, splendor and magnificent presence. Have group members look for references to God's glory in the first 11 chapters of Ezekiel. List on the board, flip chart or overhead all the ways the glory of God is described in these chapters.

Tell the group that Judah's sin caused the glory of God to depart and not return to Israel until the third Temple is built in chapter 43. **God's glory departs when His Spirit is grieved.** Discuss the following:

How can we experience God's glory in worship?

What do we do to grieve His Spirit?

How do we honor and cherish the presence of His glory?

What do we do to rob God of His glory?

SECTION TWO: GOD'S PERSON (10 MINUTES)

EZEKIEL: GOD'S WATCHMAN

Have everyone follow along as you read Ezekiel 3:17; 33:2-9.

With the whole group, list on the board, flip chart or overhead all the ways a prophet or man of God is a watchman for God's people. The list may include prayer, intercession, preaching God's Word, listening to God, resisting evil and idolatry, seeing God at work in history, fixing one's heart on God, etc.

Say: **A watchman was able to see what the enemy was doing and warn the inhabitants of incoming danger. He was also able to see what the people were doing inside the walls—both good and evil. He could warn them of sin in the camp.**

Discuss:

How can Christians be effective watchmen for one another? For the church? For their families?

OPTION TWO: (FOR A 90-MINUTE SESSION)

Visions and Parables from God (15 Minutes)

God gave Ezekiel powerful visions and parables about His glory and the future of Israel. The key text of his life is Ezekiel 1:1, "While I was among the exiles...the heavens were opened and I saw visions of God."

Divide the whole group into six small groups. Assign each group one of the following passages:

      Group One: Vision of the Cherubim (1:1-28)
      Group Two: Vision of Godlessness (8:1-16)
      Group Three: Vision of God's Glory Departing the Temple
                          (9:1—10:1-7,18,19)
      Group Four: Vision of the Burning Vine (15:1-8)

Group Five: Vision of Dry Bones (37:1-24)

Group Six: Parables and Signs (17:1-24)

Give each group a piece of poster board and felt-tip pens. Say: **Draw a picture of the vision or parable you have read in Ezekiel. Incorporate into your picture as much of the vision or parable as possible. When you have completed your picture, choose one person to explain your poster to the whole group.**

Give the groups about five minutes to do their pictures and then have each small group share their posters.

SECTION THREE: GOD'S SON (20 MINUTES)

JESUS CHRIST REVEALED AS THE SON OF MAN

Objective: To discover how Jesus is portrayed as Messiah, the Son of Man, in Ezekiel.

One of the most important titles for the Messiah in the Old Testament is introduced in Ezekiel. That title is Son of Man. Son of Man refers to a human being and the coming Messiah.

Divide the group into four small groups. Assign each group one of the following passages:

Group One: Ezekiel 3:1-19

Group Two: Ezekiel 12:1-27

Group Three: Ezekiel 21:1-17

Group Four: Ezekiel 33: 1-20

As they survey their passages, each group is to:

1. Note by each passage any way that it may apply to the coming Messiah.

2. Have each group share the passages they found pertaining to the coming Messiah and what they revealed about the Messiah.

List on the board, flip chart or overhead the passages referring to the Messiah as each group shares and ask everyone to jot down the references on their handouts. Then discuss the following:

How is the messianic title "Son of Man" fulfilled by Jesus?

PURSUING GOD (5 MINUTES)

NEXT STEPS I NEED TO TAKE

Objective: To take a realistic assessment of one's relationship with Jesus and how that relationship might grow closer in the coming week.

Ask everyone to find a partner. Have the pairs read Ezekiel 36:26-28 together. Ask the partners to complete these sentences with one another:

One new way God worked in my life when He gave me a new heart was _____.

I need His Spirit to move me to _____.

One experience of God's newness and glory in my life is _____.

PRAYER (5 MINUTES)

Objective: To pray for God's glory with a new spirit and heart.

Staying in pairs, invite them to pray for their partners in light of what has just been shared in their sentence completions.

After two minutes, bring the whole group together. Close in prayer asking for God to put a new heart and renewed spirit in each group member to empower them to live for Him. That prayer might be something like this:

Almighty God, put a new heart and renew Your Spirit in each person with new and fresh power so that all of us may keep Your laws and live totally as Your people, in Jesus' name. Amen.

Session 8 Bible *Tuck-In*™

UNDERSTANDING EZEKIEL

The purpose of this session is:

- To provide an overview of the book of Ezekiel;
- To discover how Jesus Christ is revealed as the Son of Man.

KEY VERSES

"Son of man, I [God] have made you a watchman for the house of Israel; so hear the word I speak and give them warning from me." Ezekiel 33:7

"I will give you a new heart and put a new spirit in you; I will remove from you your heart of stone and give you a heart of flesh. And I will put my Spirit in you and move you to follow my decrees and be careful to keep my laws." Ezekiel 36:26,27

"Therefore prophesy and say to [Israel]: 'This is what the Sovereign LORD says: O my people, I am going to open your graves and bring you back up from them; I will bring you back to the land of Israel. Then you, my people, will know that I am the LORD, when I open your graves and bring you up from them.'" Ezekiel 37:12,13

Group Three: Ezekiel 21:1-17
Group Four: Ezekiel 33: 1-20

- While surveying their assigned passages, each group is to:

  1. Note by each passage any way that it may apply to the coming Messiah.

  2. Have them share the passages they found pertaining to the coming Messiah and what they revealed about the Messiah.

- List on the board, flip chart or overhead what the groups share and ask everyone to jot down the references on their handout sheets.

- Then discuss the following: **How is the messianic title "Son of Man" fulfilled by Jesus?**

PURSUING GOD (5 MINUTES)

NEXT STEPS I NEED TO TAKE

- Ask everyone to find a partner. Have them read Ezekiel 36:26-28 together. Ask the partners to complete these sentences with one another:

  One new way God worked in my life when He gave me a new heart was _____

  I need His Spirit to move me to _____

  One experience of God's newness and glory in my life is _____

PRAYER (5 MINUTES)

- Staying in pairs, invite them to pray for one another in light of what has just been shared in their sentence completions. After a two minutes, bring the whole group together. Close in prayer asking for God to put a new heart and renewed spirit in each group member to empower them to live for Him.

SECTION ONE: GOD'S STORY (20 MINUTES)

GOD'S STORY IN EZEKIEL

- Greet everyone as they arrive. Tell the Bible story in Ezekiel doing the suggested activities as you come to them. Distribute the handout "God's Story In Ezekiel" to group members.

- Display an overhead transparency of the "Times of the Prophets" handout from Session 5 so that the group may see where Ezekiel is on the time line.

OPTION ONE: (FOR A 90-MINUTE SESSION)

The Glory of God (15 Minutes)

- Share that God's glory refers to His radiance, splendor and magnificent presence. Have group members look for references to God's glory in the first 11 chapters of Ezekiel. List on the board, flip chart or overhead all the ways the glory of God is described in these chapters.

- Tell the group that Judah's sin caused the glory of God to depart and not return to Israel until the third Temple is built in chapter 43. **God's glory departs when His Spirit is grieved.** Discuss the following:

  How can we experience God's glory in worship?
  What do we do to grieve His Spirit?
  How do we honor and cherish the presence of His glory?
  What do we do to rob God of His glory?

SECTION TWO: GOD'S PERSON (10 MINUTES)

EZEKIEL: GOD'S WATCHMAN

- Have everyone follow along as you read Ezekiel 3:17; 33:2-9.

- With the whole group, list on the board, flip chart or overhead all the ways a prophet or man of God is a watchman for God's people. Discuss:
  How can Christians be effective watchmen for one another? For the church? For their families?

OPTION TWO: (FOR A 90-MINUTE SESSION)

Visions and Parables from God (15 Minutes)

- Divide the whole group into six small groups. Assign each group one of the following passages from Ezekiel:

  Group One: Vision of the Cherubim (1:1-28)
  Group Two: Vision of Godlessness (8:1-16)
  Group Three: Vision of God's Glory Departing the Temple (9:1—10:1-7,18,19)
  Group Four: Vision of the Burning Vine (15:1-8)
  Group Five: Vision of Dry Bones (37:1-24)
  Group Six: Parables and Signs (17:1-24)

- Give each group poster board and felt-tip pens and instructions on how to draw their pictures.

- Give the groups about five minutes to do their pictures and have each small group share their posters.

SECTION THREE: GOD'S SON (20 MINUTES)

JESUS CHRIST REVEALED AS THE SON OF MAN

- Explain the importance of the title "the son of man."

- Divide the group into four small groups. Assign each group one of the following passages:

  Group One: Ezekiel 3:1-19
  Group Two: Ezekiel 12:1-27

GOD'S STORY IN EZEKIEL

1. While Jeremiah's ministry was concluding in Judah, the young prophet Ezekiel was already at work among the exiles in Babylon.

   Notes:

2. Ezekiel can minister to the Jews today by telling them that God will fulfill His trustworthy promises of restoring their land, their people and their temple.

   Notes:

3. To the Christian, Ezekiel reveals God's purposes for Israel which demonstrates that He is acting in history to fulfill all of His promises.

   Notes:

4. Ezekiel and Daniel were young men ministering to the exiles in Babylon. God had told of Judah's captivity in Babylon more than 100 years before it happened (see Isaiah 39:6,7; Micah 4:10). Jeremiah had foretold a seventy-year captivity (see Jeremiah 25:11,12).

   Notes:

CONTINUED

5. Central to Ezekiel's prophecies was the glory of God. Ezekiel opens with heavenly glory in a vision and ends with earthly glory of God's establishment of a new Israel and a new Temple (see Ezekiel 43:1-12).

   Notes:

6. God used Ezekiel to explain why He allowed His children to be exiled. Judah had been wicked and stiff-necked; guilty of unspeakable sin and abomination.

   Notes:

7. Ezekiel prophesied destruction of Jerusalem, the judgment against Israel's enemies, Judah's restoration and the golden age to come under the Messiah.
   Ezekiel may be divided into three sections regarding the city of Jerusalem:

   a. Pre-Siege (1—24):

   b. Siege (25—32):

   c. Post-Siege (33—48):

CONTINUED

Son of Man References and Notes in Ezekiel Referring to the Messiah:

Ezekiel 3:1-19

Ezekiel 12:1-27

Ezekiel 21:1-17

Ezekiel 33:1-20

Before the next session, read:
Sunday: Daniel the Captive (Daniel 1—2)
Monday: Nebuchadnezzar the Proud King (Daniel 3—4)
Tuesday: Belshazzar's Reign (Daniel 5; 7—8)
Wednesday: Darius's Reign (Daniel 6—9)
Thursday: God's Glory (Daniel 10)
Friday: The Conflict of Kings (Daniel 11)
Saturday: Daniel's Last Message (Daniel 12)

Understanding Daniel

The purpose of this session is:

- To provide an overview of the book of Daniel;
- To discover how Jesus Christ is revealed as the Smiting Stone.

In this session, group members will learn:

- Key truths about God's story in Daniel;
- That Jesus Christ is revealed in Daniel;
- The basic principles of God's sovereignty, His righteous judgment of the wicked and His protection of the godly;
- How to apply the truths revealed in Daniel to their own lives.

KEY VERSES

"During the night the mystery was revealed to Daniel in a vision." Daniel 2:19

"I prayed to the LORD my God and confessed: 'O Lord, the great and awesome God, who keeps his covenant of love with all who love him and obey his commands, we have sinned and done wrong. We have been wicked and have rebelled; we have turned away from your commands and laws. We have not listened to your servants the prophets, who spoke in your name to our kings, our princes and our fathers, and to all the people of the land.'" Daniel 9:4-6

BEFORE THE SESSION

- Pray for group members by name, asking the Holy Spirit to teach the spiritual truths in Daniel to them.
- Read chapter 21 in *What the Bible Is All About*.
- Prepare copies of the Session 9 handout "God's Story in Daniel."
- Check off these supplies once you have secured them:
    - ____ A chalkboard and chalk or a flip chart or an overhead projector with markers.
    - ____ Extra Bibles, pencils and paper for group members.
- If you are having a 90-minute session, carefully read the two option sections right now and pull together any supplies you need for them.
- Read the entire session and look up every passage. Have your Bible *Tuck-In*™ page ready for yourself.

- Arrive early and be ready to warmly greet each group member as he or she arrives.
- Memorize the key verses. Share them periodically and ask the group to repeat them as you teach the session.

SECTION ONE: GOD'S STORY (20 MINUTES)

GOD'S STORY IN DANIEL

Objective: To tell God's story so that Christians will apply the truths from Daniel to their own lives.

Greet everyone as they arrive. Tell the following story doing the suggested activities as you come to them. Distribute the handout "God's Story In Daniel" to all the group members.

Display an overhead transparency of the "Times of the Prophets" handout from Session 5 so that the group may see where Daniel is on the time line.

Before telling the stories, have small groups do the following mimes. Since the stories about Daniel are so well known, divide the whole group into three groups. Secretly assign each group the task of miming their story for the other two groups to see if those groups can guess the story.

> Group One: Daniel in the lions' den (6:3-24);
> Group Two: The fiery furnace (3:8-29);
> Group Three: The handwriting on the wall (5:1-29).

During the reign of Nebuchadnezzar God used Daniel to demonstrate His sovereignty over the kingdoms of this world (see Daniel 4:2,3,34,35; 6:20-22).

As mighty as Nebuchadnezzar was, his wisdom paled beside God's prophet, and his power was humbled as God drove him into the field like a beast (see Daniel 4:24-33).

With the whole group discuss:

What are some examples from history in which God has humbled mighty human leaders and nations?

God used Daniel during the reign of Belshazzar to manifest His judgment on sin and wickedness.

The king's desecration of the temple implements brought down swift judgment from God (see Daniel 5:2-6,26-30).

Ask the group to help you list on the board, flip chart or overhead the various sins of our country which could bring God's judgment down upon us. Then discuss:

What keeps us from being judged by God like Babylon?

Of what sins should our nation repent?

God used Daniel during the reign of the Persian king Darius to demonstrate that He alone was to be worshiped.

Daniel's refusal to worship idols or pray to anyone but God would bring persecution and the threat of death upon him much as in the days of the early Christians (see Daniel 6:1-22).

With the whole group discuss:

What would you do if you were asked by the government to renounce your faith in Christ and honor or worship some kind of idol?

Would you die for your faith? When is it necessary to be a martyr?

How should Christians defend themselves against unjust persecution?

God also used Daniel during the reign of Darius to show that He protects the godly.

Enemies tried to entrap Daniel. The charges against him were unjust. But there is no indication in chapter 6 that Daniel tried to defend himself. With the whole group, discuss:

If God is our refuge and defense as He was for Daniel, why do we try to defend ourselves against unjust attacks?

If we do not defend ourselves, are we foolish or simply naive?

Darius rejoiced when God delivered Daniel from the lions' den (see Daniel 6:19-28).

OPTION ONE: (FOR A 90-MINUTE SESSION)

Daniel—Book of Devotions (15 Minutes)

The book of Daniel is packed with heart-touching devotional passages for the personal Christian life. Ask everyone in the group to look at the devotional list on their handouts under the section entitled "The Book of Daniel: Devotionals for the Christian Life."

Ask them to read the passages and to complete the activities listed under each passage.

Have the group form pairs and share what they have written with their partners.

SECTION TWO: GOD'S PERSON (15 MINUTES)

DANIEL: A GODLY MAN IN A LAND OF IDOLATRY AND TREACHERY

Objective: To discover qualities in Daniel's life that group members might apply to their own lives.

Daniel made himself constantly available for God to use in mighty ways. Discover for yourself some of the qualities in Daniel's life that we might emulate in our own lives.

Have group members turn to the section on their handouts entitled "Godly Qualities in Daniel's Life." Ask them to read each passage listed and to jot down the godly qualities that Daniel had in his relationship with God. After they have taken 8 to 10 minutes to look up these passages and jot down the qualities, discuss the following with the whole group:

What one quality do Christian leaders need the most?

What would be one of the most difficult qualities for you to develop in your life?

OPTION TWO: (FOR A 90-MINUTE SESSION)

God's Power and Sovereignty Revealed in Daniel (15 Minutes)

The book of Daniel reveals God's power and universal sovereignty. That means that God reigns not just over Israel but over all the nations of the earth.

Divide the whole group into six groups. Assign each group one of the first six chapters in Daniel. Ask each group to discover what is revealed about the nature, power and sovereignty of God in their assigned chapter. Ask the groups to match what they have discovered with the following list that you have written on the board, flip chart or overhead:

> God the Keeper
> God the Revealer of Secrets
> God the Deliverer
> God the Potentate
> God the Judge
> God the All-Powerful

Summarize these revelations by saying:

Daniel 1 reveals God's power in keeping and protecting Daniel and his friends.

Daniel 2 reveals God's power in revealing Nebuchadnezzar's dream to Daniel.

Daniel 3 reveals God's power in delivering Daniel's three companions from the fiery furnace.

Daniel 4 reveals God's power in dealing with the mighty king of Babylon and demonstrating that God alone reigns over the affairs of nations.

Daniel 5 reveals God's power in His awful judgment.

Daniel 6 reveals God's power over nature in delivering Daniel from the lions.

Ask any group members who wish to share something they learned about God's nature from these revelations that would apply to their everyday lives.

SECTION THREE: GOD'S SON (15 MINUTES)

JESUS CHRIST REVEALED AS THE SMITING STONE

Objective: To discover how Jesus is portrayed as the Smiting Stone in Daniel.

Say: **In the stone cut without hands the kingdom of Christ is revealed. His kingdom shall never be destroyed, and shall bring to an end all other kingdoms. Christ will come and set up His kingdom which will last forever** (see Daniel 2:44,45).

Ask volunteers to read the following passages: Psalm 118:22; Isaiah 8:14; 28:16; Daniel 2:44,45; Zechariah 3:9.

In Nebuchadnezzar's dream, the future empires were represented by gold, silver, brass and iron. Each succeeding kingdom was weaker than the one before—Babylon, Persia, Greece and Rome. With the group discuss the following:

What examples in history do we have of empires that have opposed Jesus and have fallen or crumpled?

Which empires oppose Him today and will one day be judged?

What does our country need to do in order to recognize Jesus Christ as the only King and as having the only Kingdom?

How can Christians work this out in a multicultural, pluralistic and democratic society?

How does being a Christian affect our views of obeying unjust laws, being patriotic and becoming involved as citizens in the political process?

How does the truth of Jesus' statement "Give to Caesar what is Caesar's, and to God what is God's" (Matthew 22:21) apply both to Daniel's example and to our lives?

Where would you draw the line between serving your country and serving God?

PURSUING GOD (5 MINUTES)

NEXT STEPS I NEED TO TAKE

Objective: To take a realistic assessment of one's relationship with Jesus and how that relationship might grow closer in the coming week.

Ask group members to share one quality from Daniel's life that they admire and would like God to develop in their own lives. List these qualities on the board, flip chart or overhead. Have a time of silent prayer for about two minutes with group members individually praying for those qualities that they desire God's Spirit to increase and deepen in their lives.

PRAYER (5 MINUTES)

Objective: To pray through the prayer in Daniel 9:4-19.

With the group read through Daniel's prayer of confession. Ask various group members to volunteer brief phrases that might summarize this prayer of confession and apply it to today's culture. Write the phrases on the board, flip chart or overhead. As a group pray those phrases as a corporate prayer of confession.

Session 9 Bible *Tuck-In*™

UNDERSTANDING DANIEL

The purpose of this session is:

- To provide an overview of the book of Daniel;
- To discover how Jesus Christ is revealed as the Smiting Stone.

KEY VERSES

"During the night the mystery was revealed to Daniel in a vision." Daniel 2:19

"I prayed to the LORD my God and confessed: 'O Lord, the great and awesome God, who keeps his covenant of love with all who love him and obey his commands, we have sinned and done wrong. We have been wicked and have rebelled; we have turned away from your commands and laws. We have not listened to your servants the prophets, who spoke in your name to our kings, our princes and our fathers, and to all the people of the land.'" Daniel 9:4-6

SECTION ONE: GOD'S STORY (20 MINUTES)

GOD'S STORY IN DANIEL

- Greet everyone as they arrive. Tell the Bible story, doing the

---

How does being a Christian affect our views of obeying unjust laws, being patriotic and becoming involved as citizens in the political process?

How does the truth of Jesus' statement "Give to Caesar what is Caesar's, and to God what is God's" (Matthew 22:21) apply both to Daniel's example and our lives?

Where would you draw the line between serving your country and serving God?

PURSUING GOD (5 MINUTES)

NEXT STEPS I NEED TO TAKE

- Ask group members to share one quality from Daniel's life that they admire and would like God to develop in their own lives. List these qualities on the board, flip chart or overhead.

- Have a time of silent prayer for two minutes with group members individually praying for those qualities that they desire God's Spirit to increase and deepen in their lives.

PRAYER (5 MINUTES)

- With the whole group, read through Daniel's prayer of confession in Daniel 9:4-19. Ask various group members to volunteer brief phrases that might summarize this prayer of confession and apply it to today's culture. Write these phrases on the board, flip chart or overhead. As a group, pray those phrases as a corporate prayer of confession.

suggested activities as you come to them. Distribute the handout "God's Story In Daniel" to group members.

• Display an overhead transparency of the "Times of the Prophets" handout from Session 5 so that the group may see where Daniel is on the time line.

• Before telling the story have the three groups do their mimes from Daniel's life.

OPTION ONE: (FOR A 90-MINUTE SESSION)

Daniel—Book of Devotions (15 Minutes)

• Ask everyone in the group to turn to their handout section entitled "The Book of Daniel: Devotionals for the Christian Life."

• Ask them to read the passages and complete the activities under each passage.

• Have the group form pairs and share what they have written.

SECTION TWO: GOD'S PERSON (15 MINUTES)

DANIEL: A GODLY MAN IN A LAND OF IDOLATRY AND TREACHERY

• Have group members turn to the handout section entitled "Godly Qualities in Daniel's Life." Ask them to read each passage listed and to jot down the godly qualities that Daniel had in his relationship with God. After 8 to 10 minutes, discuss the following:

What one quality do Christian leaders need the most? What would be one of the most difficult qualities for you to develop in your life?

OPTION TWO: (FOR A 90-MINUTE SESSION)

God's Power and Sovereignty Revealed in Daniel (15 Minutes)

• The book of Daniel reveals God's power and universal **sovereignty. That means that God reigns not just over Israel but over all the nations of the earth.**

• Divide the whole group into six groups. Assign each group one of the first six chapters in Daniel. Ask each group to discover what is revealed about the nature, power and sovereignty of God in their assigned chapter. Ask the groups to match what they have discovered with the list that you have written on the board, flip chart or overhead.

• Summarize the revelations.

• Ask any group members who wish to share something they learned about God's nature from these revelations that would apply to their everyday lives.

SECTION THREE: GOD'S SON (15 MINUTES)

JESUS CHRIST REVEALED AS THE SMITING STONE

• Ask volunteers to read the following passages: Psalm 118:22; Isaiah 8:14; 28:16; Daniel 2:44,45; Zechariah 3:9.

Discuss:

What examples in history do we have of empires that have opposed Jesus and have fallen or crumpled? Which empires oppose Him today and will be judged by Him?

What does our country need to do in order to recognize Jesus Christ as the only King and as having the only Kingdom? How can Christians work this out in a multicultural, pluralistic and democratic society?

GOD'S STORY IN DANIEL

1. During the reign of Nebuchadnezzar God used Daniel to demonstrate His sovereignty over the kingdoms of this world (see Daniel 4:2,3,34,35; 6:20-22).

   Notes:

2. God used Daniel during the reign of Belshazzar to manifest His judgment on sin and wickedness.

   Notes:

3. God used Daniel during the reign of the Persian king Darius to demonstrate that He alone was to be worshiped.

   Notes:

4. God used Daniel during the reign of Darius to show that He protects the godly.

   Notes:

CONTINUED

THE BOOK OF DANIEL: DEVOTIONALS FOR THE CHRISTIAN LIFE

Instructions: Put an X on the lines to mark where you are right now. Complete the sentences.
Check any items that apply to you.

1. The surrendered life (Daniel 1:1-21)
    Right now, my life is...

    _____

    Totally surrendered   Not surrendered at all

    One area of my life that I need to surrender is...

2. Light in the midst of darkness (Daniel 2:20-22)

    I need God's light for...

3. Triumph Through Trial (Daniel 3:16-29)
    When facing a trial I feel...
    _____ Defeated before I start.
    _____ Anxious and worried.
    _____ Confident.
    _____ Fearful.
    _____ Able to face all things in Christ.
    _____ Depressed or discouraged.
    _____ Positive and hopeful.
    _____ Ready to grow.
    _____ Ready to retreat.

4. The reward of service (Daniel 5:16,17)

    I serve God and others because...

CONTINUED

5. Prayer and confidence in God (6:7-24)

My prayer life needs...

6. Confession of sin (Daniel 9:4,5,13-29)
The way I usually deal with my sin and guilt is to:
____ Confess it immediately.
____ Repress it.
____ Ignore it.
____ Feel guilty for a long while.
____ Share my confession with another Christian.
____ Other: _____

7. The wisdom of soul-winning (Daniel 12:3)

The reason I witness to others about Jesus is...

GODLY QUALITIES IN DANIEL'S LIFE
Look up each passage and then list the godly qualities that Daniel possessed in that passage:

Daniel 1:8-17

Daniel 2:27-30

CONTINUED

Daniel 5:5-17

Daniel 6:6,10-22

Daniel 9:2-7,15-17,20-23

Before the next session, read:
Sunday: Israel's Willful Ignorance (Hosea 4)
Monday: Israel's Glorious Future (Hosea 3; 14)
Tuesday: Punishment and Blessing (Joel 2)
Wednesday: The Restoration of Israel (Joel 3)
Thursday: Personal Admonitions (Amos 3:1-7; 4:6-12)
Friday: The Prophet's Intercession (Amos 7:1-17; 8:1-7)
Saturday: Future Kingdom Blessings (Amos 9:1-15)

Understanding Hosea, Joel and Amos

The purpose of this session is:
- To provide an overview of the books of Hosea, Joel and Amos;
- To discover how Jesus Christ is revealed as the Healer of the backslider; the Restorer and the heavenly Husbandman.

In this session, group members will learn:
- Key truths about God's story in Hosea, Joel and Amos;
- That Jesus Christ is revealed in Hosea, Joel and Amos;
- The basic principles of righteousness, mercy and broken covenants;
- How to apply the truths revealed in these books to their own lives.

KEY VERSES

"I will betroth you to me forever; I will betroth you in righteousness and justice, in love and compassion. I will betroth you in faithfulness, and you will acknowledge the LORD." Hosea 2:19,20

"And afterward, I will pour out my Spirit on all people. Your sons and daughters will prophesy, your old men will dream dreams, your young men will see visions." Joel 2:28

"I hate, I despise your religious feasts; I cannot stand your assemblies." Amos 5:21

"Let justice roll on like a river, righteousness like a never-failing stream!" Amos 5:24

BEFORE THE SESSION

- Pray for group members by name, asking the Holy Spirit to teach the spiritual truths in these books to them.
- Read chapter 22 in *What the Bible Is All About*.
- Prepare copies of the Session 10 handout "God's Story in Hosea, Joel and Amos."

- Check off these supplies once you have secured them:
  - ____ A chalkboard and chalk or a flip chart or an overhead projector with markers;
  - ____ Extra Bibles, pencils and paper for group members.
- If you are having a 90-minute session, carefully read the two option sections right now and pull together any supplies you need for them.
- Read the entire session and look up every passage. Have your Bible *Tuck-In*™ page ready for yourself.
- Arrive early and be ready to warmly greet each group member as he or she arrives.
- Memorize the key verses. Share them periodically and ask the group to repeat them as you teach the session.

SECTION ONE: GOD'S STORY (20 MINUTES)

GOD'S STORY IN HOSEA, JOEL AND AMOS

Objective: To tell God's story so that Christians will apply the truths in these books to their own lives.

Greet everyone as they arrive. Tell the following story, doing the suggested activities as you come to them. Distribute the handout "God's Story in Hosea, Joel and Amos" to group members.

Display an overhead transparency of the "Times of the Prophets" handout from Session 5 so that the group may see where these prophets are on the time line.

God made a covenant with Abraham and Israel at Mount Sinai for Israel to be His people, His bride. Hosea tells about a broken covenant: a broken relationship between God, the Husband, and His bride, Israel.

Have the group members look at their handouts. With the group recall God's promises in His covenants. Have them recall what they have already learned before you give them any of the following answers:

Covenant	God's Promise	Our Responsibility
Edenic (Genesis 2:15-17)	Life & provision of the Garden	To obey and not partake of the tree of the knowledge of good and evil

Adamic (Genesis 3:14-24)	Curse of death, Eve's Offspring will redeem sinful humanity	To work hard, bear children
Noahic (Genesis 8:15-22)	Will never send another flood	Sacrifice, not eat meat with blood, be fruitful
Abrahamic (Genesis 12:1-3)	Great nation, seed to bless the nations; bless Israel and be blessed; curse Israel and be cursed	Faith, obedience, circumcision
Mosaic (Exodus 20)	That Israel would be God's people	Obedience to God's law
Palestinian (Deuteronomy 31:3-16)	The Promised Land of Palestine	Not to follow after other gods
Davidic (2 Samuel 7:5-16)	Eternal household for King & Messiah; eternal Kingdom	Build God's house

In the prophets, God judges His people for breaking the old covenants and promises a new covenant. Assign the following passages to various group members and ask them to read their verses out loud: **Isaiah 24:5; Isaiah 61:8,9; Jeremiah 11:10; Jeremiah 31:31-34; Hosea 2:14-20.** Then discuss the following:
What are the promises and conditions of the new covenant that God will give?

Through Joel, God promises to pour out His Spirit so that His people can be empowered to keep His covenant and to know Him.

Joel foresaw the birth and spread of the Church beginning with the day of Pentecost in Acts 2.

Have everyone read Joel 2:28-32 and Acts 2. On the board, flip chart or overhead list all the promises in Joel. Next to each promise, list how that was fulfilled in Acts 2.

Through Amos, God declares His judgment of wickedness and His demand for righteousness and justice.

The Hebrew word for judgment is *mishpaht* meaning "to decide upon that which is righteous and just."

Read Amos 5:21-24 out loud to the group. Discuss the following:

What is the difference between true faith in God and a civil religion that compromises the truth of God and contradicts His Word?

Israel's religion became a tool of the state and so absorbed in the culture that genuine faith was lost. How can we avoid that danger today?

Through the prophets Hosea and Amos, God demands righteousness or *tsedaqah*. Righteousness goes beyond ritual and ceremony. It requires obedience to God's law and having a holy, personal and right relationship with God and other persons.

Have volunteers read Hosea 10:12; Amos 5:24, then discuss:

How can we keep our desire for righteousness (see Matthew 5:6) from becoming legalism?

OPTION ONE: (FOR A 90-MINUTE SESSION)

Understanding Joel (15 Minutes)

Divide the whole group into groups of three. Assign one person in each group to each chapter in Joel. Write on the board, flip chart or overhead:

> Joel 1: The Plague—The Warning
>
> Joel 2: The Fast—The Promise
>
> Joel 3: The Blessing—The Future.

Ask everyone to summarize his or her assigned chapter of Joel in one sentence and then share their summaries with their other group members.

Bring the whole group back together. As a group discuss:

What blessings and promises can we claim today for the Church and the saints?

SECTION TWO: GOD'S PERSON (15 MINUTES)

HOSEA: FORGIVING AND UNCONDITIONAL LOVE

Objective: To discover qualities in Hosea's life that group members might apply to their own lives.

Have everyone skim through Hosea 1—3. With the whole group, reconstruct the main elements of Hosea's story about his relationship with Gomer and list those elements on the board, flip chart or overhead. Then with the group brainstorm and list all of the qualities of unconditional love that they can think of and circle the two or three qualities that are the most important.

Say: **One of the key Hebrew words in the Old Testament referring to God's nature is *heced* which means "mercy, lovingkindness, faithfulness." The mercy and forgiving love that God demonstrates through Hosea's example is the love He shows us.**

Assign the following passages to various group members: Hosea 2:19; 4:1; 6:4; 10:12; 12:6; Joel 2:13. Have them read the passages to the whole group. After each passage is read, have volunteers complete the following sentence:

God's mercy—lovingkindness—is _____.

Discuss the following with the whole group:

How difficult would it have been for you to obey God if you had been Hosea?

How can we apply God's *heced*—mercy—in our families and marriages?

OPTION TWO: (FOR A 90-MINUTE SESSION)

Amos: The Bold Prophet (15 Minutes)

Amos was a simple shepherd from Tekoa. What were his qualities as a prophet?

Divide the whole group into three smaller groups. Assign three chapters of Amos to each group. Ask them to spend about five minutes surveying the book of

Amos looking for qualities that reflect his boldness and relationship with God. Then ask group members to share what they have discovered and list that on the board, flip chart or overhead. Compare that list to the following:

Amos was humble because he didn't hide his lowly position as a shepherd.

Amos was wise because he didn't preach over the heads of his people.

Amos was clever because he caught people's interest by judging their enemies first.

Amos was fearless because he did not tickle the ear but told the truth.

Amos was faithful because "Thus saith the Lord" was his message.

Discuss the following:

How would Amos be treated today?

What part of Amos's message is most needed today?

SECTION THREE: GOD'S SON (15 MINUTES)

JESUS CHRIST REVEALED AS THE HEALER OF THE BACKSLIDER, THE RESTORER AND THE HEAVENLY HUSBANDMAN

Objective: To discover how Jesus is portrayed in these prophetic books.

Divide the whole group into three groups. Assign each group one of the following passages: Hosea 3 and 14; Joel 3 and Amos 9. In Hosea they are to look for verses about Him healing the backslider. In Joel, they are to find verses about restoring God's people. In Amos, they are to locate verses about the Lord being a heavenly Husbandman.

With the whole group, discuss:

How is the Church like and unlike Israel or Judah as shown in Hosea, Joel and Amos?

What sins addressed in these three books does the Church need to particularly avoid?

PURSUING GOD (5 MINUTES)

NEXT STEPS I NEED TO TAKE

Objective: To take a realistic assessment of one's relationship with Jesus and how that relationship might grow closer in the coming week.

Complete the sentences on the handout under the section "Pursuing God." Ask group members to find partners and share their sentence completions together.

PRAYER (5 MINUTES)

Objective: To pray through the sentences just shared in "Pursuing God."

Ask each person to select one sentence completion to pray for with his or her partner.

Session 10 Bible *Tuck-In*™

UNDERSTANDING HOSEA, JOEL AND AMOS

The purpose of this session is:

- To provide an overview of these books;
- To discover how Jesus Christ is revealed as the Healer of the backslider, the Restorer and the heavenly Husbandman.

KEY VERSES

"I will betroth you to me forever; I will betroth you in righteousness and justice, in love and compassion. I will betroth you in faithfulness, and you will acknowledge the LORD." Hosea 2:19,20

"And afterward, I will pour out my Spirit on all people. Your sons and daughters will prophesy, your old men will dream dreams, your young men will see visions." Joel 2:28

"I hate, I despise your religious feasts; I cannot stand your assemblies." Amos 5:21

"Let justice roll on like a river, righteousness like a never-failing stream!" Amos 5:24

- Discuss the following:

How would Amos be treated today?

What part of Amos's message is most needed today?

SECTION THREE: GOD'S SON (15 MINUTES)

JESUS CHRIST REVEALED AS THE HEALER OF THE BACKSLIDER, THE RESTORER AND THE HEAVENLY HUSBANDMAN

- Divide the whole group into three groups. Assign each group one of the following passages: Hosea 3 and 14; Joel 3 and Amos 9. In Hosea they are to look for verses about God healing the backslider. In Joel, they are to find verses about restoring God's people. In Amos they are to locate verses about the Lord being a heavenly Husbandman.

- After about seven minutes of searching, have the three groups share with the whole group what they have discovered. Then discuss:

How is the Church like and unlike Israel and Judah as shown in Hosea, Joel and Amos?

What sins addressed in these three books does the Church need to particularly avoid?

PURSUING GOD (5 MINUTES)

NEXT STEPS I NEED TO TAKE

- Have pairs complete the sentences on their handouts.
- Have the partners share their sentence completions with each other.

PRAYER (5 MINUTES)

- Ask each person to select one sentence completion to pray for with his or her partner

SECTION ONE: GOD'S STORY (20 MINUTES)

GOD'S STORY IN HOSEA, JOEL AND AMOS

- Greet everyone as they arrive. Tell the Bible story, doing the suggested activities as you come to them. Distribute the handout "God's Story in Hosea, Joel and Amos" to group members.

- Display an overhead transparency of the "Times of the Prophets" handout from Session 5 so that the group may see where these prophets are on the time line.

OPTION ONE: (FOR A 90-MINUTE SESSION)

Understanding Joel (15 Minutes)

- Divide the whole group into groups of three. Assign one person in each group to each chapter in Joel. Write on the board, flip chart or overhead:

  Joel 1: The Plague—The Warning

  Joel 2: The Fast—The Promise

  Joel 3: The Blessing—The Future.

- Ask everyone to summarize his or her assigned chapter of Joel in one sentence and then share their summaries with their other group members.

- Bring the whole group back together and discuss: **What blessings and promises can we claim today for the Church and the saints?**

SECTION TWO: GOD'S PERSON (15 MINUTES)

HOSEA: FORGIVING AND UNCONDITIONAL LOVE

- Have everyone skim Hosea 1—3. Reconstruct the main elements of Hosea's story about his relationship with

— Fold —

Gomer and list those elements on the board, flip chart or overhead. Then with the group list all of the qualities of unconditional love that they can think of and circle the two or three qualities that are the most important.

- Assign the following passages to be read out loud: Hosea 2:19; 4:1; 6:4; 10:12; 12:6; Joel 2:13. After each passage is read, have volunteers complete this sentence:

  God's mercy—lovingkindness—is _____

- Discuss as a group:

  How difficult would it have been for you to obey God if you had been Hosea?

  How can we apply God's *hesed*—mercy—in our families and marriages?

OPTION TWO: (FOR A 90-MINUTE SESSION)

Amos: The Bold Prophet (15 Minutes)

- Divide the whole group into three groups. Assign three chapters of Amos to each group.

- Ask them to survey their chapters looking for qualities that reflect his boldness and relationship with God. After 5 minutes, have them share what they have discovered and list that on the board, flip chart or overhead.

- Compare that list to the following:

  Amos was humble because he didn't hide his lowly position as a shepherd; Amos was wise because he didn't preach over the heads of his people.

  Amos was clever because he caught people's interest by judging their enemies first.

  Amos was fearless because he did not tickle the ear but told the truth; Amos was faithful because "Thus saith the Lord" was his message.

GOD'S STORY IN HOSEA, JOEL AND AMOS

1. God made a covenant with Abraham and Israel at Mount Sinai for Israel to be His people, His bride. Hosea tells about a broken covenant: a broken relationship between God, the Husband, and His bride, Israel.

Covenant	God's Promise	Our Responsibility
Edenic (Genesis 2:15-17)		
Adamic (Genesis 3:14-24)		
Noahic (Genesis 8:15-22)		
Abrahamic (Genesis 12:1-3)		
Mosaic (Exodus 20)		

CONTINUED

Palestinian
(Deuteronomy 31:3-16)

Davidic
(2 Samuel 7:5-16)

2. Through Joel, God promises to pour out His Spirit so that His people can be empowered to keep His covenant and to know Him.

   Notes:

3. Through Amos, God declares His judgment of wickedness and His demand for righteousness and justice.

   Notes:

4. Through the prophets Hosea and Amos, God demands righteousness or *tsedaqah*. Righteousness goes beyond ritual and ceremony. It requires obedience to God's law and having a holy, personal and right relationship with God and other persons.

   Notes:

CONTINUED

PURSUING GOD

1. I need to repent of backsliding in the area of…

2. I need God's restoration in my life in…

3. In my life, I thank God for cultivating…

Before the next session, read:
Sunday: Doom and Deliverance (Obadiah 1-21)
Monday: A Fish Story (Jonah 1—2)
Tuesday: An Obedient Prophet (Jonah 3—4)
Wednesday: A Message to the People (Micah 1—2)
Thursday: A Message to the Rulers (Micah 3—4)
Friday: The Birth and Rejection of the King (Micah 5)
Saturday: A Message to the Chosen People (Micah 6—7)

Understanding Obadiah, Jonah and Micah

The purpose of this session is:

- To provide an overview of the books of Obadiah, Jonah and Micah;
- To discover how Jesus Christ is revealed as our Savior, our Resurrection and our Life and the Witness against rebellious nations.

In this session, group members will learn:

- Key truths about God's story in these prophetic books;
- That Jesus is revealed in Obadiah, Jonah and Micah;
- The basic principle that God loves all peoples, but that there is terrible judgment for those who choose to be His enemies;
- How to apply the truths revealed in these books to their own lives.

KEY VERSES

"The day of the LORD is near for all nations. As you have done, it will be done to you; your deeds will return upon your own head." Obadiah 15

"'In my distress I called to the LORD, and he answered me. From the depths of the grave I called for help, and [God] listened to my cry.'" Jonah 2:2

"He has showed you, O man, what is good. And what does the LORD require of you? To act justly and to love mercy and to walk humbly with your God." Micah 6:8

BEFORE THE SESSION

- Pray for group members by name, asking the Holy Spirit to teach the spiritual truths in Obadiah, Jonah and Micah to them.
- Read chapter 23 in *What the Bible Is All About*.
- Prepare copies of Session 11 handout "God's Story in Obadiah, Jonah and Micah."
- Check off these supplies once you have secured them:
    _____ A chalkboard and chalk, or a flip chart, or an overhead projector with markers.

____ Extra Bibles, pencils and paper for group members.

- If you are having a 90-minute session, carefully read the two option sections right now and pull together any supplies you need for them.
- Read the entire session and look up every passage. Have your Bible *Tuck-In*™ page ready for yourself.
- Arrive early and be ready to warmly greet each group member as he or she arrives.
- Memorize the key verses. Share them periodically and ask the group to repeat them as you teach the session.

SECTION ONE: GOD'S STORY (20 MINUTES)

GOD'S STORY IN OBADIAH, JONAH AND MICAH

Objective: To tell God's story so that Christians will apply the truths of these books to their own lives.

Greet everyone as they arrive. Tell the following story, doing the suggested activities as you come to them. Distribute the handout "God's Story in Obadiah, Jonah and Micah" to group members.

Display an overhead transparency of the "Times of the Prophets" handout from Session 5 so that the group may see where these prophets are on the time line.

The descendants of Esau—Jacob's brother—were called Edomites. For centuries they were Israel's sworn enemies. God used Obadiah to prophesy against the Edomites.

Their capital city of Petra was one of the wonders of the ancient world. Built in the cliffs of Mount Seir, Petra was believed by the Edomites to be invincible but about five years after Nebuchadnezzar sacked Jerusalem, he destroyed Petra (see Obadiah 1-4).

With the whole group discuss:

How is the fate of Edom similar to what happened to the Soviet Union?

Where should a nation's security rest?

Is it possible today for there to be peace in Israel through treaties and alliances? Why?

Through Obadiah, God spoke to Israel about her future. A key prophetic phrase is "the day of the Lord."

This is an eschatological term. Eschatology is the study of the future in God's hands. The day of the Lord refers to the final wrath and judgment of God at the end of time (see Obadiah 15).

Assign everyone in the group one or two of the following passages. If there are more group members than individual passages, assign the same passages to more than one person. Ask them to look them up and then write on their handouts what their passages say about "the day of the Lord": Isaiah 2:2; 13:6; 34:8, Jeremiah 46:10; Lamentations 2:22; Ezekiel 13:5; 30:3; Amos 5:18; Zephaniah 1:8,18; 2:2,3; Malachi 4:5; 1 Thessalonians 5:2; 2 Peter 3:10.

Ask everyone to share what they have learned with the whole group. Encourage everyone to jot down on their handouts what they have learned.

Jonah was a "type" of Israel. A "type" is a symbolic representation of one thing which has characteristics similar to another. That means that Jonah acted toward Assyria as Israel would respond to the nations of the earth (see Jonah 1:3).

God told Jonah to go to Nineveh—the capital city of Assyria and Israel's enemy— and preach repentance. Jonah ran away in the opposite direction. He had no desire to preach in the capital of Assyria, much less to see them repent and spared by God (see Jonah 1:1,2).

Discuss as a group:

If God told you to take the gospel to an enemy with the possibility of losing your personal freedom or your life, what would you do?

When an enemy repents, what feelings do you have?

With the whole group, put the following statements in the correct chronological order (These statements are arranged in the correct order of events in Jonah. The student handout has the events in random order. After the group has put the events in order, the following correct order can be given.):

1. Jonah was called to a world mission; so was Israel.
2. Jonah refused to obey God and fulfill his mission; so did Israel.
3. Jonah was punished by being cast into the sea; Israel by being scattered among the nations.
4. Jonah was preserved; so was a remnant of Israel.
5. Jonah repented and was cast out of the fish; Israel was restored to her former position.
6. Jonah finally obeyed God and returned to perform his mission; Israel in obedience shall become a witness to all the earth.
7. Jonah was blessed because Nineveh was brought to salvation; Israel shall be blessed as the nations and Gentiles are converted and saved through Jesus Christ.

Discuss the following:

How has Israel fulfilled these prophesies?

What is happening now in Israel that makes her a witness to the nations?

The focus of Jonah should not be the fish but a people. Jonah focuses on the truth that God loves all people, not just Israel.

God expects obedience. When Jonah disobeyed God, then he reaped the consequences of God's correction (see Jonah 1:17-2:10).

Ask everyone to read Hebrews 12:4-13, then discuss:

How does God correct believers when they disobey Him?

Micah lived in the country twenty miles outside of Jerusalem. God used him to denounce the social sins of his day—the unfair treatment of the poor, the corruption of justice and the oppression by the government (see Micah 1:3-7).

Divide the whole group into three small groups. Assign one of the following sections to each group. Ask them to summarize the central prophetic warning and God's promise found in their assigned section in one sentence.

Group 1: Micah 1—2
Group 2: Micah 3—5
Group 3: Micah 6—7

Have each group share what they have discovered with the whole group.

OPTION ONE: (FOR A 90-MINUTE SESSION)

The Essentials of Authentic Faith (15 Minutes)

Have three concordances available. Divide the whole group into three groups. Give each group a concordance for their research. Assign each group one of the following attitudes of authentic faith from Micah 6:8:

Group 1: Act justly (justice, righteousness, righteous).
Group 2: Love mercy (mercy, lovingkindness).
Group 3: Walk humbly with God (humble, meek, proud).

Tell each group to look up the key words following each heading. Have one person in each group jot down what the prophets say about these themes.

Have the recorders share what their group learned. Write the main ideas on the board, flip chart or overhead. Discuss with the whole group:

How should Christians live righteously in our culture?

How can we show mercy?

What do we need to do with our pride and arrogance?

SECTION TWO: GOD'S PERSON (15 MINUTES)

JONAH: THE RELUCTANT PROPHET

Objective: To discover qualities in Jonah's life from which group members might learn about obeying God.

Jonah lived during the reign of Jeroboam II in the Northern Kingdom of Israel (see 2 Kings 14:25). Jonah was patriotic and hated Israel's enemy, Assyria. Let's see how we might be like Jonah.

Brainstorm with the whole group all the options Jonah may have had when God told him to go to Nineveh. List those options on the board, flip chart or overhead. For each option, brainstorm and list why group members think Jonah did not take the option to obey God.

Read Jonah 2, then discuss as a whole group:

Was Jonah's repentance in Jonah 2 sincere or forced by God?

Then read Jonah 3:1-3 and discuss:

Why did Jonah get depressed when Nineveh repented?

OPTION TWO: (FOR A 90-MINUTE SESSION)

Sins of the Nation (15 Minutes)

Divide the group into groups of four. Ask each group to skim through Micah and make a list of all the sins condemned by God in Micah. Have the small groups share which of the sins on the list are most prevalent in our culture today. Give about eight minutes for this. Some of the sins that they should note are: idolatry (1:7; 6:16); covetousness (2:2); oppression (2:2; 7:3); violence (3:10; 6:12; 7:2); encouraging false prophets (2:6); corruption of princes, rulers and leaders (3:1-3); corruption of

prophets, spiritual preachers and spokesmen (3:5-7); corruption of priests (3:11); bribery (3:9,11; 7:3); dishonesty (6:10,11).

With the whole group discuss:

Which national sins mentioned in Micah do we face in our culture today?

What can Christians do in response to these sins?

(Some responses might be to pray, repent, be more active as citizens in the political processes to change and remove sin from our governmental agencies.)

SECTION THREE: GOD'S SON (15 MINUTES)

JESUS CHRIST REVEALED AS OUR SAVIOR, OUR RESURRECTION AND OUR LIFE AND THE WITNESS AGAINST REBELLIOUS NATIONS

Objective: To discover how Jesus is revealed in these prophetic books.

Ask everyone to find a partner. On the handout, turn to the section entitled "The Messiah and the Kingdom of God in Micah." Give each pair about seven minutes to complete the handout section and then discuss the following with the whole group:

How is God's kingdom as described in Micah like the kingdom of God that Jesus talks about in the Sermon on the Mount?

What aspects of God's kingdom are we experiencing today?

What is Jesus doing now to increase His kingdom in our midst?

Jesus refers to the sign of Jonah as the only sign the Jews will receive to confirm that He is the Messiah (see Matthew 12:39-45). **What signs do people look for today?**

PURSUING GOD (5 MINUTES)

NEXT STEPS I NEED TO TAKE

Objective: To take a realistic assessment of one's relationship with Jesus and how that relationship might grow closer in the coming week.

Form pairs and ask partners to summarize the story of Jonah. Have them share a time in their lives when they ran from something they knew God was asking them to do. Invite them to make a verbal commitment with their partners of how they will respond in the future when God asks them to do something that they do not want to do.

PRAYER (5 MINUTES)

Objective: To focus prayer for one another on Micah 6:8 and Jonah 2.

Invite everyone to read Micah 6:8, and share with his or her partner which requirement from God they need to follow through on the most during the coming week: act justly, love mercy, or walk humbly with God. Once they have both shared which of these is most needed in their lives and why, have the partners pray for one another.

Have everyone turn to Jonah 2. In closing, read Jonah's prayer in unison.

Session 11 Bible *Tuck-In*™

UNDERSTANDING OBADIAH, JONAH AND MICAH

The purpose of this session is:

- To provide an overview of these books;
- To discover how Jesus Christ is revealed as our Savior, our Resurrection and our Life, and the Witness against rebellious nations.

KEY VERSES

"The day of the LORD is near for all nations. As you have done, it will be done to you; your deeds will return upon your own head." Obadiah 15

"'In my distress I called to the LORD, and he answered me. From the depths of the grave I called for help, and [God] listened to my cry.'" Jonah 2:2

"He has showed you, O man, what is good. And what does the LORD require of you? To act justly and to love mercy and to walk humbly with your God." Micah 6:8

SECTION THREE: GOD'S SON (15 MINUTES)

JESUS CHRIST REVEALED AS OUR SAVIOR, OUR RESURRECTION AND OUR LIFE AND THE WITNESS AGAINST REBELLIOUS NATIONS

- Ask everyone to find a partner. Give each pair about seven minutes to complete the handout section "The Messiah and God's Kingdom in Micah" and then discuss the following with the whole group: **How is God's kingdom as described in Micah like the kingdom of God that Jesus talks about in the Sermon on the Mount? What aspects of God's kingdom are we experiencing today? What is Jesus doing now to increase His kingdom in our midst?** Jesus refers to the sign of Jonah as the only sign the Jews will receive to confirm that He is the Messiah (see Matthew 12:39-45). **What signs do people look for today? What do they need to see?**

PURSUING GOD (5 MINUTES)

NEXT STEPS I NEED TO TAKE

- Form pairs and ask partners to summarize the story of Jonah. Have them share a time in their lives when they ran from something they knew God was asking them to do. Invite them to make a verbal commitment with their partners about how they will respond in the future when God asks them to do something they do not want to do.

PRAYER (5 MINUTES)

- Invite everyone to read Micah 6:8 and share with his or her partner which requirement from God they need to follow through on the most during the coming week. Once they have both shared, have the partners pray for one another.
- Have everyone turn to Jonah 2. In closing, read Jonah's prayer in unison.

SECTION ONE: GOD'S STORY (20 MINUTES)

GOD'S STORY IN OBADIAH, JONAH AND MICAH

- Greet everyone as they arrive. Tell the Bible Story, doing the suggested activities as you come to them. Distribute the handout "God's Story in Obadiah, Jonah and Micah" to group members.

- Display an overhead transparency of the "Times of the Prophets" handout from Session 5 so that the group may see where these prophets are on the time line.

OPTION ONE: (FOR A 90-MINUTE SESSION)

The Essentials of Authentic Faith (15 Minutes)

- Divide the whole group into three groups. Give each group a concordance. Assign each group one of the following attitudes of authentic faith from Micah 6:8:

  Group 1: Act justly (justice, righteousness, righteous).
  Group 2: Love mercy (mercy, lovingkindness).
  Group 3: Walk humbly with God (humble, meekness, pride).

- Tell each group to look up the key words following each heading. Have one person in each group jot down what the prophets say about these themes. Have the recorders share what their group learned. Write the main ideas on the board, flip chart or overhead. Discuss: **How should Christians live righteously in our culture? How can we show mercy? What do we need to do with our pride and arrogance?**

160

---Fold---

SECTION TWO: GOD'S PERSON (15 MINUTES)

JONAH: THE RELUCTANT PROPHET

- Brainstorm with the whole group all the options Jonah may have had when God told him to go to Nineveh. List those options on the board, flip chart or overhead. For each option, brainstorm and list why group members think Jonah did not take the option to obey God.

- Read Jonah 2 and then discuss as a whole group.

- Read Jonah 3:1-3 and ask: **Why did Jonah get depressed when Nineveh repented?**

OPTION TWO: (FOR A 90-MINUTE SESSION)

Sins of the Nation (15 Minutes)

- Divide the group into groups of four. Ask each group to skim through Micah and make a list of all the sins condemned by God in Micah. Have them share which of the sins on the list are most prevalent in our culture today. Some of the sins that they should note are: idolatry (1:7; 6:16); covetousness (2:2); oppression (2:2; 7:3); violence (3:10; 6:12; 7:2); encouraging false prophets (2:6); corruption of princes, rulers and leaders (3:1-3); corruption of prophets, spiritual preachers and spokesmen (3:5-7); corruption of priests (3:11); bribery (3:9,11; 7:3); dishonesty (6:10,11)

- With the whole group discuss: **Which national sins mentioned in Micah do we face in our culture today? What can Christians do in response to these sins?**

GOD'S STORY IN OBADIAH, JONAH AND MICAH

1. The descendants of Esau—Jacob's brother—were called Edomites. For centuries they were Israel's sworn enemies. God used Obadiah to prophesy against the Edomites.

   Notes:

2. Through Obadiah, God spoke to Israel about her future. A key prophetic phrase is "the day of the Lord."

   The day of the Lord is…

3. Jonah was a "type" of Israel. A "type" is a symbolic representation of one thing which has characteristics similar to another. That means that Jonah acted toward Assyria as Israel would respond to the nations of the earth (Jonah 1:3).

   _____ Jonah was punished by being cast into the sea; Israel by being scattered among the nations.

   _____ Jonah finally obeyed God and returned to perform his mission; Israel in obedience shall become a witness to all the earth.

   _____ Jonah was blessed when Nineveh was brought to salvation; Israel shall be blessed as the nations and Gentiles are converted and saved through Jesus Christ.

   _____ Jonah was preserved; so was a remnant of Israel.

   _____ Jonah repented and was cast out of the fish; Israel was restored to her former position.

   _____ Jonah was called to a world mission; so was Israel.

   _____ Jonah refused to obey God and fulfill his mission; so did Israel.

4. The focus of Jonah should not be the fish but a people. Jonah focuses on the truth that God loves all people, not just Israel.

   Notes:

CONTINUED

5. Micah lived in the country twenty miles outside of Jerusalem. God used him to denounce the social sins of his day—the unfair treatment of the poor, the corruption of justice and the oppression by the government.

Notes:

THE MESSIAH AND THE KINGDOM OF GOD IN MICAH
List the qualities of the kingdom of God found in:

Micah 4:1-5

Matthew 5:1-12

Read the following passages and jot down what they say about the coming Messiah.

Micah 2:12,13

Micah 4:1,7

CONTINUED

Micah 5:2

Before the next session, read:
Sunday: The Judge and the Verdict (Nahum 1)
Monday: The Execution (Nahum 2—3)
Tuesday: Habakkuk's Complaint (Habakkuk 1)
Wednesday: God's Reply (Habakkuk 2)
Thursday: Habakkuk's Song (Habakkuk 3)
Friday: Coming Judgments (Zephaniah 1—2)
Saturday: The Kingdom Blessings (Zephaniah 3)

Understanding Nahum, Habakkuk and Zephaniah

The purpose of this session is:

- To provide an overview of the books of Nahum, Habakkuk and Zephaniah;
- To discover how Jesus Christ is revealed as our Stronghold in the day of trouble, the God of our salvation and a jealous Lord.

In this session, group members will learn:

- Key truths about God's story in Nahum, Habakkuk and Zephaniah;
- That Jesus Christ is revealed in Nahum, Habakkuk and Zephaniah;
- The basic principle that God is a righteous Judge who has pronounced His judgment on the wicked and yet offers salvation to all who come to Him.
- How to apply the truths revealed in these books to their own lives.

KEY VERSES

"The LORD is slow to anger and great in power; the LORD will not leave the guilty unpunished.... The LORD is good, a refuge in times of trouble. He cares for those who trust him." Nahum 1:3,7

"How long, O LORD, must I call for help, but you do not listen? Or cry out to you, 'Violence!' but you do not save?" Habakkuk 1:2

"The LORD your God is with you, he is mighty to save. He will take great delight in you, he will quiet you with his love, he will rejoice over you with singing." Zephaniah 3:17

BEFORE THE SESSION

- Pray for group members by name, asking the Holy Spirit to teach the spiritual truths in Nahum, Habakkuk and Zephaniah to them.
- Read chapter 24 in *What the Bible Is All About*.

- Prepare copies of Session 12 handout "God's Story in Nahum, Habakkuk and Zephaniah."
- Check off these supplies once you have secured them:
  - ____ A chalkboard and chalk or a flip chart or an overhead projector with markers;
  - ____ Felt-tip pens and three sheets of poster board;
  - ____ Extra Bibles, pencils and paper for group members.
- If you are having a 90-minute session, carefully read the two option sections right now and pull together any supplies you need for them.
- Read the entire session and look up every passage. Have your Bible *Tuck-In*™ page ready for yourself.
- Arrive early and be ready to greet warmly each group member as he or she arrives.
- Memorize the key verses. Share them periodically and ask the group to repeat them as you teach the session.

SECTION ONE: GOD'S STORY (20 MINUTES)

GOD'S STORY IN NAHUM, HABAKKUK AND ZEPHANIAH

Objective: To tell God's story so that Christians will apply the truths in these books to their own lives.

Greet everyone as they arrive. Tell the following story, doing the suggested activities as you come to them. Distribute the handout "God's Story in Nahum, Habakkuk and Zephaniah" to group members.

Display an overhead transparency of the "Times of the Prophets" handout from Session 5 so that the group may see where these prophets are on the time line.

God's message through Nahum was about the destruction of Nineveh and the deliverance of His people.

About 150 years after the revival that Jonah witnessed, Nineveh was again filled with evil. Unheeded mercy brings judgment. Assyria had been built by violence and war. They worshiped the idol, Asshur. God utterly destroyed Nineveh as He promised through Nahum (see Nahum 1:8).

Divide the whole group into groups of three. Ask each person within each small group to survey one of the chapters in Nahum and then share his or her responses to the following within the small group:

- **An important or favorite verse from that chapter;**
- **The theme of that chapter in one sentence;**
- **One thing that God is saying to that person in his or her assigned chapter.**

In Nahum, God reveals that He is both Judge and Executioner.

God pronounced His judgment and delivered His punishment. Nineveh's fate was complete destruction. The truth of reaping what is sown applies to both pagans and God's people. Nineveh had sown violence and she reaped violence. (See Nahum 3.)

The Bible speaks often of the ultimate judgment of God. With the whole group, discuss:

Does a Christian have anything to fear at the final judgment of God? (See Matthew 25:31-46 and Revelation 20.)

How should the knowledge about the judgment of God motivate us to share the gospel with the lost?

We know little about Habakkuk except that he asked God many questions and received God's answers.

He complained to God and heard God's response of both judgment and hope. (See Habakkuk 2:1-4.)

Divide the whole group into three groups. Give each group felt-tip pens and a sheet of poster board. Assign one of the chapters of Habakkuk to each group and have them survey the assigned chapter. Have each group make a poster that represents the theme of that chapter.

Tell each group to also choose one verse from their assigned chapter that they wish to memorize. Have them repeat that verse without looking at the Bible at least three times. Some verses that might be chosen are Habakkuk 1:2; 2:4; 3:19.

When the groups have completed their posters, ask one person from each group to share what the poster means and to share their memory verse.

In Zephaniah, God reveals Himself as both loving and severe.

Through Zephaniah God promised to bring a faithful remnant of His people back to Judah. He also promised that the heathen would be converted and that one day humanity could worship God everywhere not just in Jerusalem. (See Zephaniah 3:17-20.)

In Zephaniah the day of the Lord is once again revealed. Ask the whole group to go back into their groups of three and ask each person to choose one chapter in Zephaniah to skim over. Ask them to complete each of the sentences on their handouts and share with the others in their small group:

God's judgment will _____.

God's promise is _____.

OPTION ONE: (FOR A 90-MINUTE SESSION)

God's Terrible Judgment (15 Minutes)

With the whole group, read through Nahum 1. Have them brainstorm God's qualities as both Judge and Father that are revealed in this chapter. Then list the qualities on the board, flip chart or overhead. Some of the things that may be discovered are:

God as Judge is…	God as Father is…
Jealous	Slow to anger
Vengeful	Good
Furious	A Stronghold in the day of trouble
Indignant	Knows those who trust Him
Great in power	
Will not acquit the wicked	

Next make a list of the various aspects of God's verdict against Nineveh. (Nineveh was condemned to destruction, captured while her defenders were drunk, had her name blotted out and God dug her grave.)

After making these lists, discuss the following:

Do people today understand the terrible judgment of God?

How can we balance the truth that God is both Judge and Father?

How does knowing that God is a jealous God affect your relationship with Him?

How can we communicate that God is the Judge and still speak of His love and mercy?

SECTION TWO: GOD'S PERSON (15 MINUTES)

ZEPHANIAH: USING A PRIVILEGED POSITION FOR GOD

Objective: To discover qualities in Zephaniah's life that might teach group members about obeying God.

Have everyone in the group read Zephaniah 1 and discover all the facts that they can about Zephaniah's life. List what they discover on the board, flip chart or overhead. (Zephaniah came from a royal family. He had a privileged position in Judah. He used that position to speak God's Word to God's people.)

Have the group look at the checklist on the handout under the section "What Keeps Us from Speaking God's Word?" After everyone has completed the checklist, as a group rank the order of the list from the most common hindrance to the least common one.

OPTION TWO: (FOR A 90-MINUTE SESSION)

God Judges the Nations (15 Minutes)

Nineveh is a "type" of all nations that turn their backs on God. In our day, proud civilizations are staking everything upon the strength of manpower, treaties, the U.N., bombs and machines instead of turning to the Prince of Peace.

Ask everyone in the group to survey Nahum and find one verse that really speaks to the world situation today. Ask them to share the verse they chose and why they chose it.

Have a prayer of intercession for the nations of the earth. Pray for repentance and salvation to come to the world.

Section Three: God's Son (15 Minutes)

Jesus Christ Revealed as Our Stronghold in the Day of Trouble, the God of Our Salvation and a Jealous God

Objective: To discover how Jesus is revealed in these books.

While Jesus is often portrayed as the meek servant of the Lord, He is also the King who judges. Those who do not accept Him as Savior and Lord will face Him as their Judge. These three prophets highlight the truth of God's wrath and judgment as well as salvation.

Assign the following passages to be read by various group members: John 5:22,30; 8:15,16; 9:39; 2 Timothy 4:1; 1 Peter 4:5; Jude 14,15; Revelation 19:11. Have everyone complete the following sentence. List their various responses on the board, flip chart or overhead:

Jesus as Judge is _____.

Pursuing God (5 Minutes)

Next Steps I Need to Take

Objective: To take a realistic assessment of one's relationship with Jesus and how that relationship might grow closer in the coming week.

Have each person survey the three books and choose one verse from each book that particularly speaks to him or her. Ask them to share with a partner the verses they found and why they have been touched by those verses.

Invite them to share how they feel God is leading them to grow in their relationship with Jesus through their chosen verses.

Prayer (5 Minutes)

Objective: To pray together the verses just shared in "Pursuing God."

Have the whole group form a circle and have volunteers pray using one verse that they chose in the "Pursuing God" activity as a closing prayer.

Session 12 Bible *Tuck-In*™

UNDERSTANDING NAHUM, HABAKKUK AND ZEPHANIAH

The purpose of this session is:

- To provide an overview of the books of Nahum, Habakkuk and Zephaniah;
- To discover how Jesus Christ is revealed as our Stronghold in the day of trouble, the God of our salvation and a jealous Lord.

KEY VERSES

"The LORD is slow to anger and great in power; the LORD will not leave the guilty unpunished.... The LORD is good, a refuge in times of trouble. He cares for those who trust him." Nahum 1:3,7

"How long, O LORD, must I call for help, but you do not listen? Or cry out to you, 'Violence!' but you do not save?" Habakkuk 1:2

"The LORD your God is with you, he is mighty to save. He will take great delight in you, he will quiet you with his love, he will rejoice over you with singing." Zephaniah 3:17

SECTION THREE: GOD'S SON (15 MINUTES)

JESUS CHRIST REVEALED AS THE STRONGHOLD IN THE DAY OF TROUBLE, THE GOD OF OUR SALVATION AND A JEALOUS GOD

- While Jesus is often portrayed as the meek servant of the Lord, He is also the King who judges. Those who do not accept Him as Savior and Lord will face Him as Judge.
- Assign the following passages to be read by various group members: John 5:22,30; 8:15,16; 9:39; 2 Timothy 4:1; 1 Peter 4:5; Jude 14,15; Revelation 19:11. Have everyone complete the following sentence. List their various responses on the board, flip chart or overhead:

Jesus as Judge is _____

PURSUING GOD (5 MINUTES)

NEXT STEPS I NEED TO TAKE

- Have each person survey the three books and choose one verse from each book that particularly speaks to him or her. Ask them to share with a partner the verses they found and why they have been touched by those verses.
- Invite them to share how they feel God is leading them to grow in their relationship with Jesus through their chosen verses.

PRAYER (5 MINUTES)

- Have the whole group form a circle and have volunteers pray using a verse they chose in the "Pursuing God" activity as a closing prayer.

SECTION ONE: GOD'S STORY (20 MINUTES)

GOD'S STORY IN NAHUM, HABAKKUK AND ZEPHANIAH

- Greet everyone as they arrive. Tell the Bible story in these books, doing the suggested activities as you come to them. Distribute the handout "God's Story in Nahum, Habakkuk and Zephaniah" to all the group members.

- Display an overhead transparency of the "Times of the Prophets" handout from Session 5 so that the group may see where these prophets are on the time line.

OPTION ONE: (FOR A 90-MINUTE SESSION)

God's Terrible Judgment (15 Minutes)

- With the whole group, read through Nahum 1. Have the them brainstorm God's qualities as both Judge and Father that are revealed in this chapter. Then list the qualities on the board, flip chart or overhead. Some of the things that may be discovered are:

God as Judge is...
Jealous
Vengeful
Furious
Indignant
Great in power
Will not acquit the wicked

God as Father is...
Slow to anger
Good
A Stronghold in
   the day of trouble
Knowing them that trust Him

- Next make a list of the various aspects of God's verdict against Nineveh. (Nineveh was condemned to destruction, captured while her defenders were drunk, had her name blotted out, and God dug her grave.)

- After making these lists, discuss the following:

Do people today understand the terrible judgment of God?

How can we balance the truth that God is both Judge and Father?

How does knowing that God is a jealous God affect your relationship with Him?

How can we communicate that God is the ultimate Judge and still speak of His love and mercy?

SECTION TWO: GOD'S PERSON (15 MINUTES)

ZEPHANIAH: USING A PRIVILEGED POSITION FOR GOD

- Have everyone in the group read Zephaniah 1 and discover all the facts that they can about Zephaniah's life. List what they discover on the board, flip chart or overhead. (Zephaniah came from a royal family. He had a privileged position in Judah. He used that position to speak God's Word to God's people.)

- Have the group look at the checklist on the handout under the section "What Keeps Us from Speaking God's Word?" After everyone has completed the checklist, as a group rank the order of the list from the most common hindrance to the least common one.

OPTION TWO: (FOR A 90-MINUTE SESSION)

God Judges the Nations (15 Minutes)

- Ask everyone in the group to survey Nahum and find one verse that really speaks to the world situation today. Ask them to share the verse they chose and why they chose it.

- Have a prayer of intercession for the nations of the earth. Pray for repentance and salvation to come to the world.

God's Story in Nahum, Habakkuk and Zephaniah

1. God's message through Nahum was about the total destruction of Nineveh and the deliverance of His people.

   Notes:

2. In Nahum, God reveals that He is both Judge and Executioner.

   Notes:

3. We know little about Habakkuk except that he asked God many questions and received God's answers.

   Memory verse:

   Notes:

4. In Zephaniah, God reveals Himself as both loving and severe.
   God's judgment will _____.
   God's promise is _____.

   Notes:

CONTINUED

WHAT KEEPS US FROM SPEAKING GOD'S WORD?

Rank the following list in order of what hinders you from speaking God's truth and Word to others with 1 being the most hindrance and 7 being the least:

____ Fear of rejection

____ Uncertainty

____ God's Word may be unpleasant or uncomfortable

____ My desire not to offend others

____ I might lose status or favor

____ Speaking God's truth might be costly for me

____ Other: _____

Before the next session, read:

Sunday: Haggai's Message (Haggai 1—2)

Monday: Visions (Zechariah 1—6)

Tuesday: Fasts (Zechariah 7—8)

Wednesday: Restoration of Judah and Israel (Zechariah 9—11)

Thursday: The Messiah (Zechariah 12—14)

Friday: Sins of Priest and People (Malachi 1—2)

Saturday: Message of Hope (Malachi 3—4)

Understanding Haggai, Zechariah and Malachi

The purpose of this session is:
- To provide an overview of the books of Haggai, Zechariah and Malachi;
- To discover how Jesus Christ is revealed as the Desire of all nations, the Righteous Branch and the Sun of righteousness.

In this session, group members will learn:
- Key truths about God's story in Haggai, Zechariah and Malachi;
- That Jesus Christ is revealed in these books;
- The basic principles of God's promises of future blessings for His people and the coming Messiah;
- How to apply the truths revealed in these books to their own lives.

KEY VERSES

"Now this is what the LORD Almighty says: 'Give careful thought to your ways. You have planted much, but have harvested little. You eat, but never have enough. You drink, but never have your fill. You put on clothes, but are not warm. You earn wages, only to put them in a purse with holes in it. You expected much, but see, it turned out to be little. What you brought home, I blew away. Why?' declares the LORD Almighty. 'Because of my house, which remains a ruin, while each of you is busy with his own house.'" Haggai 1:5,6,9

"'This is the word of the LORD to Zerubbabel: "Not by might nor by power, but by my Spirit," says the LORD Almighty.'" Zechariah 4:6

"See, I will send you the prophet Elijah before that great and dreadful day of the LORD comes. He will turn the hearts of the fathers to their children, and the hearts of the children to their fathers; or else I will come and strike the land with a curse." Malachi 4:5,6

BEFORE THE SESSION

- Pray for group members by name, asking the Holy Spirit to teach the spiritual truths in these books to them.

- Read chapter 25 in *What the Bible Is All About*.
- Prepare copies of Session 13 handout "God's Story in Haggai, Zechariah and Malachi."
- Check off these supplies once you have secured them:
  - ____ A chalkboard and chalk, or a flip chart, or an overhead projector with markers;
  - ____ Extra Bibles, pencils and paper for group members.
  - ____ Have donuts for the entire group. Get a variety so that the group that discovers the most prophecies in the book of Zechariah can have first choice of their favorite donuts.
- If you are having a 90-minute session, carefully read the two option sections right now and pull together any supplies you need for them.
- Read the entire session and look up every passage. Have your Bible *Tuck-In*™ page ready for yourself.
- Arrive early and be ready to warmly greet each group member as he or she arrives.
- Memorize the key verses. Share them periodically and ask the group to repeat them as you teach the session.

SECTION ONE: GOD'S STORY (20 MINUTES)

GOD'S STORY IN HAGGAI, ZECHARIAH AND MALACHI

Objective: To tell God's story so that Christians will apply the truths in Haggai, Zechariah and Malachi to their own lives.

Greet everyone as they arrive. Tell the following story, doing the suggested activities as you come to them. Distribute the handout "God's Story in Haggai, Zechariah and Malachi" to all the group members.

Display an overhead transparency of the "Times of the Prophets" handout from Session 5 so that the group may see where these prophets are on the time line.

God spoke to His people through Haggai, urging them to rebuild the Temple after the exile (Haggai 1:7-9).

Read Haggai 1:7-9 to the whole group, and then discuss:
Do churches spend too much on buildings? Why or why not?

How can churches develop a righteous balance between building facilities and doing ministry?

God spoke through Zechariah, revealing powerful visions of God's future blessings and the coming Messiah. There are more visions in Zechariah than in any other prophetic book (see Zechariah 1:1).

Have everyone in the group skim the first six chapters of Zechariah and find as many visions as they can. Then list those visions that they have found on the board. Here are the texts that introduce each of his visions: 1:1; 1:7; 1:18; 2:1; 3:1; 4:1; 5:5; 6:1.

Discuss the following questions:

How does God give visions today to His people?

How can we know that a vision comes from God?

Through Malachi, God revealed the sins of God's priests and people and promised the coming messenger for the Messiah and the kingdom of God.

In Malachi 4:2, God reveals that the coming Messiah will be the "Sun of Righteousness."

Divide the group into two smaller groups. Assign Malachi 3 to one group and Malachi 4 to the other. Ask them to look for characteristics of the coming age of the Messiah and to list them. Invite both groups to share their findings with the whole group.

OPTION ONE: (FOR A 90-MINUTE SESSION)

Giving to God (15 Minutes)

A major focus of Malachi is giving to God.

Divide the group into three groups. Assign the following passages to the groups and ask them to summarize in a few sentences the teachings about giving found in these passages.

Group One: Leviticus 27:30-33; Psalm 112:9; Malachi 3:8-12

Group Two: Matthew 6:19-24; Luke 6:38;

Group Three: 2 Corinthians 8:8-15; 9:6-15.

After the groups share their summaries, discuss:

What blessings have you received from giving back to the Lord a portion of what He has given to you?

What should be the benchmark for a Christian's giving?

What keeps people from giving cheerfully to the Lord?

Is the tithe the best standard for Christian giving? Why or why not?

SECTION TWO: GOD'S PERSON (15 MINUTES)

HAGGAI: A ZEALOT FOR GOD'S HOUSE

Objective: To discover qualities in Haggai's life that teach about obeying God.

Haggai seemed to have one overarching concern as a prophet: He loved God's house. He was also the first voice heard after the exile.

With the whole group, make three lists on the board as they survey the book of Haggai.

1. List everything that Haggai says about the Temple.
2. List everything that Haggai mentions as God's promises of blessings for His people.
3. List all the reasons why we should be excited about the house of God.

Invite different people to share their testimonies about the blessings received...

- When they have given to building God's house.
- When they have worked on or repaired God's house.
- When they have worshiped in God's house.

OPTION TWO: (FOR A 90-MINUTE SESSION)

Confronting Sin (15 Minutes)

Have a discussion with the whole group about the following:

What are the major sins of God's people in the Church today?

What are the major sins of the leaders and ministers in the Church today?

Divide everyone into two groups. Have one group survey Malachi 1:1—2:9 and list the sins of the priests that are found in their passage and circle any sins especially tempting to today's ministers. Ask the other group to survey Malachi 2:10—3:18 and list the sins of the people that are found in their passage and circle any that they are especially tempting to God's people today.

With the whole group discuss:

How can we resist these sins today in the Church?

As a group, have a prayer time asking God for the strength and power to resist these sins today.

SECTION THREE: GOD'S SON (15 MINUTES)

JESUS CHRIST REVEALED AS THE COMING MESSIAH IN ZECHARIAH

Objective: To see how Jesus is revealed in Zechariah as the coming Messiah.

There are more prophecies about the Messiah in Zechariah than any other Old Testament book except Isaiah.

Divide the whole group into groups of three. Tell them that there are 11 prophecies about the Messiah in Zechariah. Tell the groups that they have about seven or eight minutes to find all 11. Ask them to write the references and a brief phrase to describe each prophecy on their handouts. After the time is up, bring them back together and have them share what they have found. The group that has found the most prophecies wins the first choice of donuts.

Here is a list of the prophecies to check against those found by the group members:

> Christ the Branch—3:8
> Christ my Servant—3:8
> Jesus' entry into Jerusalem on a colt—9:9
> Christ the good Shepherd—9:16; 11:4-9
> Christ the smitten Shepherd—13:7
> Christ betrayed for 30 pieces of silver—11:12,13
> Jesus' hands pierced—12:10
> Christ's people saved—12:10; 13:1
> Christ wounded in the house of His friends—13:6
> Christ's return on the Mount of Olives—14:3-8
> Christ's return and coronation—Zechariah 14

PURSUING GOD (5 MINUTES)

NEXT STEPS I NEED TO TAKE

Objective: To take a realistic assessment of one's relationship with Jesus and how that relationship might grow closer in the coming week.

Turn to the handout and read over the list of sins from Malachi. Have group members form pairs and ask each person to share which one they need to resist most in their lives. Then have the partners pray for one another.

PRAYER (5 MINUTES)

Objective: To give thanksgiving for what has been learned in this study.

Ask each person to share:

One thing that I have learned in this study that has blessed me is _____.

Close in a circle of prayer, with anyone who wishes sharing a sentence prayer of thanksgiving. As the leader, be the last one to close this time of prayer.

Session 13 Bible *Tuck-In*™

UNDERSTANDING HAGGAI, ZECHARIAH AND MALACHI

The purpose of this session is:

- To provide an overview of the books of Haggai, Zechariah and Malachi;

- To discover how Jesus Christ is revealed as the Desire of all nations; the Righteous Branch and the Sun of righteousness.

KEY VERSES

"Now this is what the LORD Almighty says: 'Give careful thought to your ways. You have planted much, but have harvested little. You eat, but never have enough. You drink, but never have your fill. You put on clothes, but are not warm. You earn wages, only to put them in a purse with holes in it. You expected much, but see, it turned out to be little. What you brought home, I blew away. Why?' declares the LORD Almighty. 'Because of my house, which remains a ruin, while each of you is busy with his own house.'" Haggai 1:5,6,9

"'This is the word of the LORD to Zerubbabel: "Not by might nor by power, but by my Spirit," says the LORD Almighty.'" Zechariah 4:6

---

of the people and circle any that are especially tempting to God's people today.

- With the whole group discuss:

  How can we resist these sins today in the Church?

- As a group, have a prayer time asking God for the strength and power to resist these sins today.

SECTION THREE: GOD'S SON (15 MINUTES)

JESUS CHRIST REVEALED AS THE COMING MESSIAH IN ZECHARIAH

- Divide the whole group into groups of three. Tell them that there are 11 prophecies about the Messiah in Zechariah. Tell the groups that they have about seven or eight minutes to find all 11. Ask them to write down the references and a brief phrase to describe each prophecy on their handouts. Have the whole group share what they have found.

PURSUING GOD (5 MINUTES)

NEXT STEPS I NEED TO TAKE

- Read the list of sins from Malachi. Form pairs and ask each person to share which sin they need to resist most in their lives. Then have the partners pray for one another.

PRAYER (5 MINUTES)

- Ask each person to share: **One thing that I have learned in this study that has blessed me is _____.**

- Close in a circle of prayer, with anyone who wishes sharing a sentence prayer of thanksgiving. As the leader, be the last one to close this time of prayer.

"See, I will send you the prophet Elijah before that great and dreadful day of the LORD comes. He will turn the hearts of the fathers to their children, and the hearts of the children to their fathers; or else I will come and strike the land with a curse." Malachi 4:5,6

SECTION ONE: GOD'S STORY (20 MINUTES)

GOD'S STORY IN HAGGAI, ZECHARIAH AND MALACHI

- Greet everyone as they arrive. Tell the Bible story, doing the suggested activities as you come to them. Distribute the handout "God's Story in Haggai, Zechariah and Malachi" to group members.

- Display an overhead transparency of the "Times of the Prophets" handout from Session 5 so that the group may see where these prophets are on the time line.

OPTION ONE: (FOR A 90-MINUTE SESSION)

Giving to God (15 Minutes)

- Divide the group into three groups. Assign the following passages to the groups and ask them to summarize in a few sentences the teachings about giving found in these passages.

  Group One: Leviticus 27:30-33; Psalm 112:9;
                Malachi 3:8-12;
  Group Two: Matthew 6:19-24; Luke 6:38;
  Group Three: 2 Corinthians 8:8-15; 9:6-15.

- After the groups share their summaries, discuss:
  What blessings have you received from giving back to the Lord a portion of what He has given to you?

  What should be the benchmark for a Christian's giving? What keeps people from giving cheerfully to the Lord? Is the tithe the best standard for Christian giving? Why or why not?

SECTION TWO: GOD'S PERSON (15 MINUTES)

HAGGAI: A ZEALOT FOR GOD'S HOUSE

- With the whole group make three lists on the board, flip chart or overhead as you survey the book of Haggai.
  1. List everything that Haggai says about the Temple.
  2. List everything that Haggai mentions as being God's promises of blessings for His people.
  3. List all the reasons why we should be excited about the house of God.

- Invite different people to share their testimonies about blessings received...

  When they have given to building God's house.
  When they have worked on or repaired God's house.
  When they have worshiped in God's house.

OPTION TWO: (FOR A 90-MINUTE SESSION)

Confronting Sin (15 Minutes)

- Have a discussion with the whole group about the following: **What are the major sins of God's people in the Church today? What are the major sins of the leaders and ministers in the Church today?**

- Divide everyone into two groups. Have one group survey Malachi 1:1—2:9 and list the sins of the priests and circle any sins especially tempting to today's ministers. Ask the other group to survey Malachi 2:10—3:18 and list the sins

GOD'S STORY IN HAGGAI, ZECHARIAH AND MALACHI

1. God spoke to His people through Haggai, urging them to rebuild the Temple after the exile.

   Notes:

2. God spoke through Zechariah, revealing powerful visions of God's future blessings and the coming Messiah. There are more visions in Zechariah than in any other prophetic book.

   Notes:

3. Through Malachi, God revealed the sins of God's priests and people and promised the coming messenger for the Messiah and the kingdom of God.

   Notes:

RESISTING THE SINS DESCRIBED IN MALACHI
Check those sins that trouble you most in your own life or the life of the Church:

_____ Spiritless, routine worship

_____ Evil associations—negative relationships

_____ Questioning God's justice

_____ Robbing God of tithes and offerings

_____ Impatience in waiting

CONTINUED

Before the next session or the start of the next quarter of this study, read:
Sunday: The King Christ Jesus (Matthew 2:1-12; 21:1-11
Monday: The Servant Christ Jesus (Mark 10:35-45; 2:1-22)
Tuesday: The Man Christ Jesus (Luke 4:1-13; John 19:4-13)
Wednesday: The God-Man (John 1:1-18; 3:1-16)
Thursday: Our Redeemer, Jesus Christ (John 19:16-42)
Friday: The Master, Jesus Christ (Matthew 4:18-25)
Saturday: Our Master, Jesus Christ (John 21:1-17)

Bible Study Plans
Leader Instructions

As leader, photocopy the following Study Plan pages to distribute to your group. Copy the pages in duplex format so they can be easily inserted inside a Bible. Group members have the option of following a one-year plan or a two-year plan.

When you introduce the Study Plan to your group, refer to the information on the "Introduction to Study Chart" page to stimulate interest and communicate the value of this Bible Study Plan. If you have never completed such a plan yourself, join the group in committing to follow through on the monthly readings.

Should much of the current month already be gone, instruct them to simply make the "First Month" on the chart include the rest of this month and next month. Also, if there are any months in the year (e.g., December) when a person knows his or her schedule may not allow time for continuing the study plan, suggest that month be left off the chart and the name of the following month written in its place. During that "vacation" month a person may select one or more favorite sections of Scripture (e.g., Psalms, Proverbs, 1 John) in which to do devotional reading until the schedule is back to normal and the study plan can resume. It is better to plan on taking an extra month or two to complete the study than to get discouraged and quit should reading fall behind.

NOTE: If some people have doubts that they will successfully complete the Bible Study Plan, share a few tips to help them keep going should their determination waver:

1. Tell a friend what you are setting out to do and ask him or her to pray for you and regularly check with you on your progress. Making yourself accountable to someone else will help you maintain your pace and help you apply what you learn.

2. Enlist a friend to join you in the plan. Meeting together regularly to talk and to pray about what you have learned is both beneficial and motivational. Ask God to help you apply one principle you read about each day to your walk with Him.

3. Promise yourself some rewards for completing stages of the plan. You may enjoy anticipating a favorite treat each time you complete a suggested reading goal or all the suggested reading for a month. Also,

think of something special to do at the end of three months or six months or the full year. For example, why not plan a "celebration" to which you will invite a few close friends? Invite them out for dinner or dessert and include a brief explanation of some of the benefits you have gained from your Bible reading and prayer.

4. Pray regularly, telling God your doubts about "sticking it out." Ask Him for help in sticking with the daily readings and for help in understanding how He wants you to apply His Word to your life.

Bible Study Plan
Introduction to
Study Chart

As valuable as a group study is, there is no substitute for systematic, personal Bible study and prayer to grow in your walk with Christ. The plan outlined here will make Bible reading spiritually enriching as well as help deepen your understanding of the Bible both as the history of God's people and as the remarkable unified Book of God's Plan for all humanity. By following this plan, you can read through the Bible in a year, using the helpful guidance contained in *What the Bible Is All About*.

Some people become discouraged in reading the Bible from beginning to end. Some Old Testament sections are difficult to understand and even more difficult to apply to life today. Therefore, this plan lets you spend time each month in three different sections of the Bible: Old Testament Law and History, Old Testament Poetry and Prophecy, and the New Testament. The monthly Bible passages are of similar length rather than trying to complete a book by an arbitrary date. Thus, some pages in *What the Bible Is All About* are listed as resources in more than one month.

This study plan is flexible, giving you some structure and goals but allowing you to study in the way that fits you best, perhaps even varying your approach throughout the year. For example:

- Rather than giving daily assignments that may be burdensome, this plan gives monthly guidelines, letting you set the pace.
- You may prefer to set aside time every day for Bible study. Or you might enjoy reading in longer time blocks several times a week.
- You might favor the variety that comes by reading from each of the three main sections at each study session. Or you may elect to complete the month's study of each section separately.
- You might want to read the recommended sections of *What the Bible Is All About* before starting to read the Bible portions. Or you may choose to read the Bible first and then use *What the Bible Is All About* to help you understand what you have read.
- You can decide when to start your study. Keep the chart on the following pages in your Bible or in your copy of *What the Bible Is All About*. As you complete a month's suggested reading, mark the reference on the chart as an indication of your progress.

One-Year Bible Study Plan

What the Bible Is All About Chart

FIRST MONTH:

Old Testament: Law and History
Genesis 1—37 _____ *WTBIAA* pp. 13-40 _____
Old Testament: Poetry and Prophecy
Job 1—42 _____ *WTBIAA* pp. 173-185 _____
New Testament
Matthew 1—20 _____ *WTBIAA* pp. 337-357 _____

SECOND MONTH:

Old Testament: Law and History
Genesis 38—Exodus 25 _____ *WTBIAA* pp. 40-49 _____
Old Testament: Poetry and Prophecy
Psalm 1—62 _____ *WTBIAA* pp. 187-191 _____
New Testament
Matthew 21—Mark 8 _____ *WTBIAA* pp. 357-371 _____

THIRD MONTH:

Old Testament: Law and History
Exodus 26—Leviticus 23 _____ WTBIAA pp. 49-59 _____
Old Testament: Poetry and Prophecy
Psalm 63—117 _____ *WTBIAA* pp. 191-193 _____
New Testament
Mark 9—Luke 6 _____ *WTBIAA* pp. 371-387 _____

FOURTH MONTH:

Old Testament: Law and History
Leviticus 24—Numbers 28 _____ *WTBIAA* pp. 59-71 _____
Old Testament: Poetry and Prophecy
Psalm 118—Proverbs 18 _____ *WTBIAA* pp. 193-199 _____
New Testament
Luke 7—22 _____ *WTBIAA* pp. 387-391 _____

FIFTH MONTH:

Old Testament: Law and History
Numbers 29—Deuteronomy 30 _____ *WTBIAA* pp. 71-78 _____
Old Testament: Poetry and Prophecy
Proverbs 19—Isaiah 8 _____ *WTBIAA* pp. 199-217 _____
New Testament
Luke 23—John 13 _____ *WTBIAA* pp. 391-406 _____

SIXTH MONTH:

Old Testament: Law and History
Deuteronomy 31—Judges 8 _____ *WTBIAA* pp. 78-106 _____
Old Testament: Poetry and Prophecy
Isaiah 9—43 _____ *WTBIAA* pp. 217-221 _____
New Testament
John 14—Acts 11 _____ *WTBIAA* pp. 406-422 _____

SEVENTH MONTH:

Old Testament: Law and History
Judges 9—1 Samuel 21 _____ *WTBIAA* pp. 106-118 _____
Old Testament: Poetry and Prophecy
Isaiah 44—Jeremiah 6 _____ *WTBIAA* pp. 221-229 _____
New Testament
Acts 12—Romans 1 _____ *WTBIAA* pp. 422-434 _____

EIGHTH MONTH:

Old Testament: Law and History
1 Samuel 22—1 Kings 2 _____ *WTBIAA* pp. 118-136 _____
Old Testament: Poetry and Prophecy
Jeremiah 7—38 _____ *WTBIAA* pp. 229-234 _____
New Testament
Romans 2—1 Corinthians 11 _____ *WTBIAA* pp. 434-453 _____

NINTH MONTH:

Old Testament: Law and History
1 Kings 3—2 Kings 10 _____ *WTBIAA* pp. 136-143 _____
Old Testament: Poetry and Prophecy
Jeremiah 39—Ezekiel 15 _____ *WTBIAA* pp. 234-250 _____
New Testament
1 Corinthians 12—Ephesians 6 _____ *WTBIAA* pp. 453-490 _____

Tenth Month:

Old Testament: Law and History
2 Kings 11—1 Chronicles 17 _____ *WTBIAA* pp. 143-145 _____
Old Testament: Poetry and Prophecy
Ezekiel 16—45 _____ *WTBIAA* pp. 250-253 _____
New Testament
Philippians 1—Philemon _____ *WTBIAA* pp. 491-559 _____

Eleventh Month:

Old Testament: Law and History
1 Chronicles 18—2 Chronicles 31 _____ *WTBIAA* pp. 145-146 _____
Old Testament: Poetry and Prophecy
Ezekiel 46—Amos 9 _____ *WTBIAA* pp. 253-292 _____
New Testament
Hebrews 1—2 Peter 3 _____ *WTBIAA* pp. 561-607 _____

Twelfth Month:

Old Testament: Law and History
2 Chronicles 32—Esther 10 _____ *WTBIAA* pp. 146-171 _____
Old Testament: Poetry and Prophecy
Obadiah 1—Malachi 4 _____ *WTBIAA* pp. 293-334 _____
New Testament
1 John 1—Revelation 22 _____ *WTBIAA* pp. 609-636 _____

Two-Year Bible Study Plan

What the Bible Is All About Chart

FIRST MONTH:

Old Testament: Law and History
Genesis 1—21 _____ *WTBIAA* pp. 13-40 _____
Old Testament: Poetry and Prophecy
Job 1—20 _____ *WTBIAA* pp. 173-182 _____
New Testament
Matthew 1—11 _____ *WTBIAA* pp. 337-353 _____

SECOND MONTH:

Old Testament: Law and History
Genesis 22—37 _____ *WTBIAA* p. 40 _____
Old Testament: Poetry and Prophecy
Job 21—42 _____ *WTBIAA* pp. 182-185 _____
New Testament
Matthew 12—20 _____ *WTBIAA* pp. 353-357 _____

THIRD MONTH:

Old Testament: Law and History
Genesis 38—Exodus 6 _____ *WTBIAA* pp. 40-45 _____
Old Testament: Poetry and Prophecy
Psalm 1—33 _____ *WTBIAA* pp. 187-189 _____
New Testament
Matthew 21—27 _____ *WTBIAA* pp. 357-360 _____

FOURTH MONTH:

Old Testament: Law and History
Exodus 7—25 _____ *WTBIAA* pp. 45-49 _____
Old Testament: Poetry and Prophecy
Psalm 34—66 _____ *WTBIAA* pp. 189-191 _____
New Testament
Matthew 28—Mark 8 _____ *WTBIAA* pp. 360-376 _____

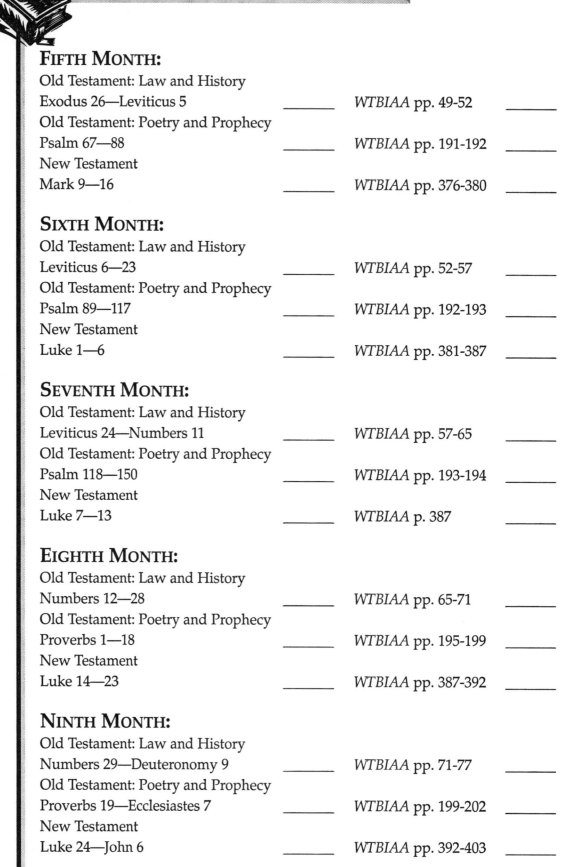

FIFTH MONTH:

Old Testament: Law and History
Exodus 26—Leviticus 5 _____ *WTBIAA* pp. 49-52 _____
Old Testament: Poetry and Prophecy
Psalm 67—88 _____ *WTBIAA* pp. 191-192 _____
New Testament
Mark 9—16 _____ *WTBIAA* pp. 376-380 _____

SIXTH MONTH:

Old Testament: Law and History
Leviticus 6—23 _____ *WTBIAA* pp. 52-57 _____
Old Testament: Poetry and Prophecy
Psalm 89—117 _____ *WTBIAA* pp. 192-193 _____
New Testament
Luke 1—6 _____ *WTBIAA* pp. 381-387 _____

SEVENTH MONTH:

Old Testament: Law and History
Leviticus 24—Numbers 11 _____ *WTBIAA* pp. 57-65 _____
Old Testament: Poetry and Prophecy
Psalm 118—150 _____ *WTBIAA* pp. 193-194 _____
New Testament
Luke 7—13 _____ *WTBIAA* p. 387 _____

EIGHTH MONTH:

Old Testament: Law and History
Numbers 12—28 _____ *WTBIAA* pp. 65-71 _____
Old Testament: Poetry and Prophecy
Proverbs 1—18 _____ *WTBIAA* pp. 195-199 _____
New Testament
Luke 14—23 _____ *WTBIAA* pp. 387-392 _____

NINTH MONTH:

Old Testament: Law and History
Numbers 29—Deuteronomy 9 _____ *WTBIAA* pp. 71-77 _____
Old Testament: Poetry and Prophecy
Proverbs 19—Ecclesiastes 7 _____ *WTBIAA* pp. 199-202 _____
New Testament
Luke 24—John 6 _____ *WTBIAA* pp. 392-403 _____

TENTH MONTH:

Old Testament: Law and History
Deuteronomy 10—30 _____ *WTBIAA* pp. 77-78 _____
Old Testament: Poetry and Prophecy
Ecclesiastes 8—Isaiah 8 _____ *WTBIAA* pp. 202-217 _____
New Testament
John 7—13 _____ *WTBIAA* pp. 403-406 _____

ELEVENTH MONTH:

Old Testament: Law and History
Deuteronomy 31—Joshua 14 _____ *WTBIAA* pp. 78-91 _____
Old Testament: Poetry and Prophecy
Isaiah 9—27 _____ *WTBIAA* pp. 217-219 _____
New Testament
John 14—Acts 2 _____ *WTBIAA* pp. 406-418 _____

TWELFTH MONTH:

Old Testament: Law and History
Joshua 15—Judges 8 _____ *WTBIAA* pp. 91-101 _____
Old Testament: Poetry and Prophecy
Isaiah 28—43 _____ *WTBIAA* pp. 219-221 _____
New Testament
Acts 3—11 _____ *WTBIAA* pp. 418-422 _____

THIRTEENTH MONTH:

Old Testament: Law and History
Judges 9—1 Samuel 2 _____ *WTBIAA* pp. 101-112 _____
Old Testament: Poetry and Prophecy
Isaiah 44—59 _____ *WTBIAA* p. 221 _____
New Testament
Acts 12—20 _____ *WTBIAA* pp. 422-425 _____

FOURTEENTH MONTH:

Old Testament: Law and History
1 Samuel 3—21 _____ *WTBIAA* pp. 112-118 _____
Old Testament: Poetry and Prophecy
Isaiah 60—Jeremiah 6 _____ *WTBIAA* pp. 221-229 _____
New Testament
Acts 21—Romans 1 _____ *WTBIAA* pp. 425-434 _____

FIFTEENTH MONTH:

Old Testament: Law and History
1 Samuel 22—2 Samuel 12 _____ *WTBIAA* pp. 118-130 _____
Old Testament: Poetry and Prophecy
Jeremiah 7—23 _____ *WTBIAA* p. 229 _____
New Testament
Romans 2—14 _____ *WTBIAA* pp. 434-442 _____

SIXTEENTH MONTH:

Old Testament: Law and History
2 Samuel 13—1 Kings 2 _____ *WTBIAA* pp. 130-136 _____
Old Testament: Poetry and Prophecy
Jeremiah 24—38 _____ *WTBIAA* pp. 229-234 _____
New Testament
Romans 15—1 Corinthians 11 _____ *WTBIAA* pp. 442-453 _____

SEVENTEENTH MONTH:

Old Testament: Law and History
1 Kings 3—16 _____ *WTBIAA* pp. 136-141 _____
Old Testament: Poetry and Prophecy
Jeremiah 39—52 _____ *WTBIAA* pp. 234-240 _____
New Testament
1 Corinthians 12—2 Cor. 10 _____ *WTBIAA* pp. 453-461 _____

EIGHTEENTH MONTH:

Old Testament: Law and History
1 Kings 17—2 Kings 10 _____ *WTBIAA* pp. 142-143 _____
Old Testament: Poetry and Prophecy
Lamentations 1—Ezekiel 15 _____ *WTBIAA* pp. 240-250 _____
New Testament
2 Corinthians 11—Ephesians 6 _____ *WTBIAA* pp. 461-490 _____

NINETEENTH MONTH:

Old Testament: Law and History
2 Kings 11—1 Chronicles 1 _____ *WTBIAA* pp. 143-145 _____
Old Testament: Poetry and Prophecy
Ezekiel 16—29 _____ *WTBIAA* pp. 250-253 _____
New Testament
Philippians 1—1 Thessalonians 5 _____ *WTBIAA* pp. 491-523 _____

TWENTIETH MONTH:

Old Testament: Law and History
1 Chronicles 2—17   _____   *WTBIAA* pp. 145-146   _____
Old Testament: Poetry and Prophecy
Ezekiel 30—45   _____   *WTBIAA* p. 253   _____
New Testament
2 Thessalonians 1—Philemon   _____   *WTBIAA* pp. 525-559   _____

TWENTY-FIRST MONTH:

Old Testament: Law and History
1 Chronicles 18—2 Chronicles 8   _____   *WTBIAA* pp. 145-146   _____
Old Testament: Poetry and Prophecy
Ezekiel 46—Daniel 12   _____   *WTBIAA* pp. 253-272   _____
New Testament
Hebrews 1—13   _____   *WTBIAA* pp. 561-571   _____

TWENTY-SECOND MONTH:

Old Testament: Law and History
2 Chronicles 9—31   _____   *WTBIAA* p. 146   _____
Old Testament: Poetry and Prophecy
Hosea 1—Amos 6   _____   *WTBIAA* pp. 273-290   _____
New Testament
James 1—2 Peter 3   _____   *WTBIAA* pp. 573-607   _____

TWENTY-THIRD MONTH:

Old Testament: Law and History
2 Chronicles 32—Nehemiah 3   _____   *WTBIAA* pp. 146-153   _____
Old Testament: Poetry and Prophecy
Amos 7—Habakkuk 3   _____   *WTBIAA* pp. 290-314   _____
New Testament
1 John 1—Revelation 8   _____   *WTBIAA* pp. 609-628   _____

TWENTY-FOURTH MONTH:

Old Testament: Law and History
Nehemiah 4—Esther 10   _____   *WTBIAA* pp. 153-171   _____
Old Testament: Poetry and Prophecy
Zephaniah 1—Malachi 4   _____   *WTBIAA* pp. 314-334   _____
New Testament
Revelation 9—22   _____   *WTBIAA* pp. 628-636   _____

CERTIFICATE OF COMPLETION

This is to certify that

_____
Name

has completed the course, *What the Bible Is All About 102 Old Testament: Job—Malachi*

on this day _____ .

_____
Signed

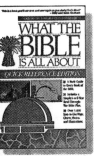
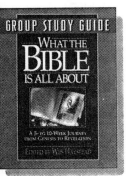
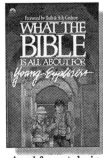
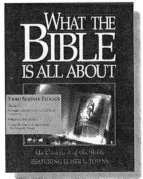

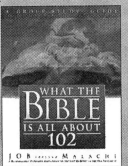
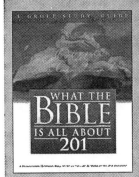
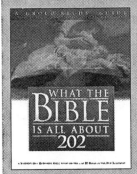